Letters from Bencoolen, 1823 - 1828

Government House and Council House, Bencoolen, 1799.
Aquatint, India Office Records

Letters from Bencoolen
1823 - 1828

Thomas Day and William Day

with an introduction
by
James Trelawny Day

Hardinge Simpole

Hardinge Simpole Publishing,
The Roan,
Kilkerran,
KA19 8LS,
Scotland,
United Kingdom

admin@hardingesimpole.co.uk
http://www.hardingesimpole.co.uk

First published in June 2008

ISBN-10 1 84382 202 4
ISBN-13 978 1 84382 202 8

To Mrs Peter Barker, (*née* Day)
for her help and encouragement

Charles Day and Family in 1820.
Courtesy of J C L Day

Preface

I have known of the existence of the 'Bencoolen letters' for many years and have always thought they were worthy of a wider audience and I am therefore very grateful to Mrs Peter Barker (*née* Day), my relation, for her permission and encouragement to publish the letters in book form. Mrs Barker and I are both great great grandchildren of Charles Day (1772-1846), to whom the letters are addressed.

In preparing the letters for publication I have had to make some minor adjustments to the text but have kept these to an absolute minimum in order to preserve the unique character of the correspondence. The letters, written in fine copper plate handwriting, are like long conversational pieces with few full stops and hardly any paragraphs, (this was probably to save paper). In order to make them more digestible I have broken down the longer passages into paragraphs and have, where necessary, introduced additional commas to make the sense of a passage more intelligible on first reading. The actual content of the letters has not been altered and in general the spelling, although sometimes amusing, has been left as in the original letters if the meaning is plain; the exception to this is where two adjacent letters in a word have obviously been transposed.

In setting out the background to the letters in the Introduction I have used many sources and these are listed in the Bibliography. I would also like to record my thanks for the great assistance I have received during my researches from many friends and relations, amongst whom I would like to mention in particular Dudley Underwood for all the research he has undertaken on my behalf, Vyvyen Brendon for her encouragement and advice on publishing, John Day for allowing me to use the portrait of Charles Day and Family and the letter in Appendix A, and Tricia Davis for her great forbearance in putting up with interminable expositions of how best to proceed. I would also like to thank the many public libraries and record offices without whose help none of this book would have been possible. Principal amongst these are the India Office Records (British Library), the Guildhall Library, the Public Record Office, the Society of Genealogists, the Oxfordshire and Berkshire Record Offices, and the Southampton Archives. In particular, however, I would like to mention Professor John Bastin's book, "The British in West Sumatra, 1685 - 1825", which has been invaluable as a source of information on Bencoolen, and also to record his encouragement many years ago to undertake this project.

Finally, as a footnote to this family saga, perhaps it is worth mentioning that Bencoolen, or Bengkulu as it is now known, which was once a small fever-ridden settlement on the west coast of Sumatra, is now a city of over a million inhabitants.

James Trelawny Day
May 2008

Contents

Preface *vii*
List of Illustrations *xi*
Introduction *xv*

Letter 1 **3**
from Thomas Day, dated 28 Feb 1823, received Nov 1823
Letter 2 **9**
from William Day, dated 29 Nov 1823, received May 1824
- concerning the death of Thomas
Letter 3 **13**
from Thomas Day, dated 26 Oct 1823,
- sent with William's letter of 29 Nov, together with accounts of 'Botany Bay' plantation (Appendix B)
Letter 4 **18**
from William Day, dated 6 Dec 1823, received May 1824
- together with copies of letters to and from the Secretary to the Government re administration of Thomas's estate
Letter 5 **27**
from William Day, dated 24 Dec 1824
- regarding the transfer of the settlement to the Dutch
Letter 6 **37**
from William Day, dated 18 Feb 1825
Letter 7 **40**
from William Day, dated 19 Feb 1825
- regarding his daughter by a native woman
Letter 8 **49**
from William Day dated 23 March 1825
- together with a copy of William's will and a letter from Messrs Ferguson & Co regarding an assignment of opium
Letter 9 **59**
from William Day, dated 10 Nov 1825
- together with accounts of 'Combong' and 'Botany Bay' plantations (Appendix C)
Letter 10 **66**
from William Day, dated 16 Jan 1826, received Aug 1826
- regarding employment by the Dutch

Letter 11 **70**
from William Day, dated 14 April 1826
Letter 12 **77**
from William Day, dated 10 Sep 1826
- regarding Dutch maladministration
Letter 13 **82**
from William Day, dated 23 Oct 1826
- regarding discharge from Dutch service
Letter 14 **84**
from William Day, dated 25 July 1827
- addressed to Mrs Day
Letter 15 **88**
from William Day, dated 28 July 1827
- regarding the possibility of going to Singapore, together with accounts of 'Combong' plantation (Appendix D)
Letter 16 **103**
from William Day, dated 20 Nov 1827, received May 1828
- regarding visit to Singapore together with note concerning a shipment of spices
Letter 17 **108**
from William Day, dated 31 May 1828, received Mar 1829
- together with accounts of 'Combong' plantation (Appendix E)
Appendix A -
Letter from Robert Samuel Perreau to his daughters, Eliza Henrietta and Francis Mary Perreau, July 1810.
Appendix B -
Accounts of 'Botany Bay' plantation sent with Letter 3, Oct 1823
Appendix C -
Accounts of 'Combong' and 'Botany Bay' plantations sent with Letter 9, Nov 1825
Appendix D -
Accounts of 'Combong' plantation sent with Letter 15, Jul 1827
Appendix E - Accounts of 'Combong' plantation sent with Letter 17, May 1828

Notes
Bibliography *146*

List of Illustrations

Government House and Council House, Bencoolen, 1799. *Aquatint, India Office Records*	*frontispiece*
Charles Day and Family in 1820. *Courtesy of J C L Day*	*vi*
Map of Indian Ocean	*xii*
East India House 1817 . *India Office Records*	*xiv*
Early Day Armorial China c. 1750	*xxix*
Ockwells Manor, Berks, c1450. *Courtesy of Country Life*	*xxi*
Stone Hall, Wallingford, Oxon	*xxi*
Fort St George (Madras) c. 1750. *Engraving after van Ryne, India Office Records*	*xxii*
Sir Stamford Raffles 1817. *Oil painting by G F Joseph ARA,* *Copyright National Portrait Gallery, London*	*xxx*
Spear Hall in 1850. *Courtesy of Mrs Peter Barker (née Day).*	*xxxvii*
Page from a typical letter from William Grant Day, 1823. *Southampton Archives*	*xxxviii*
Day, Perreau and Cooper Family Tree	*xlvi*

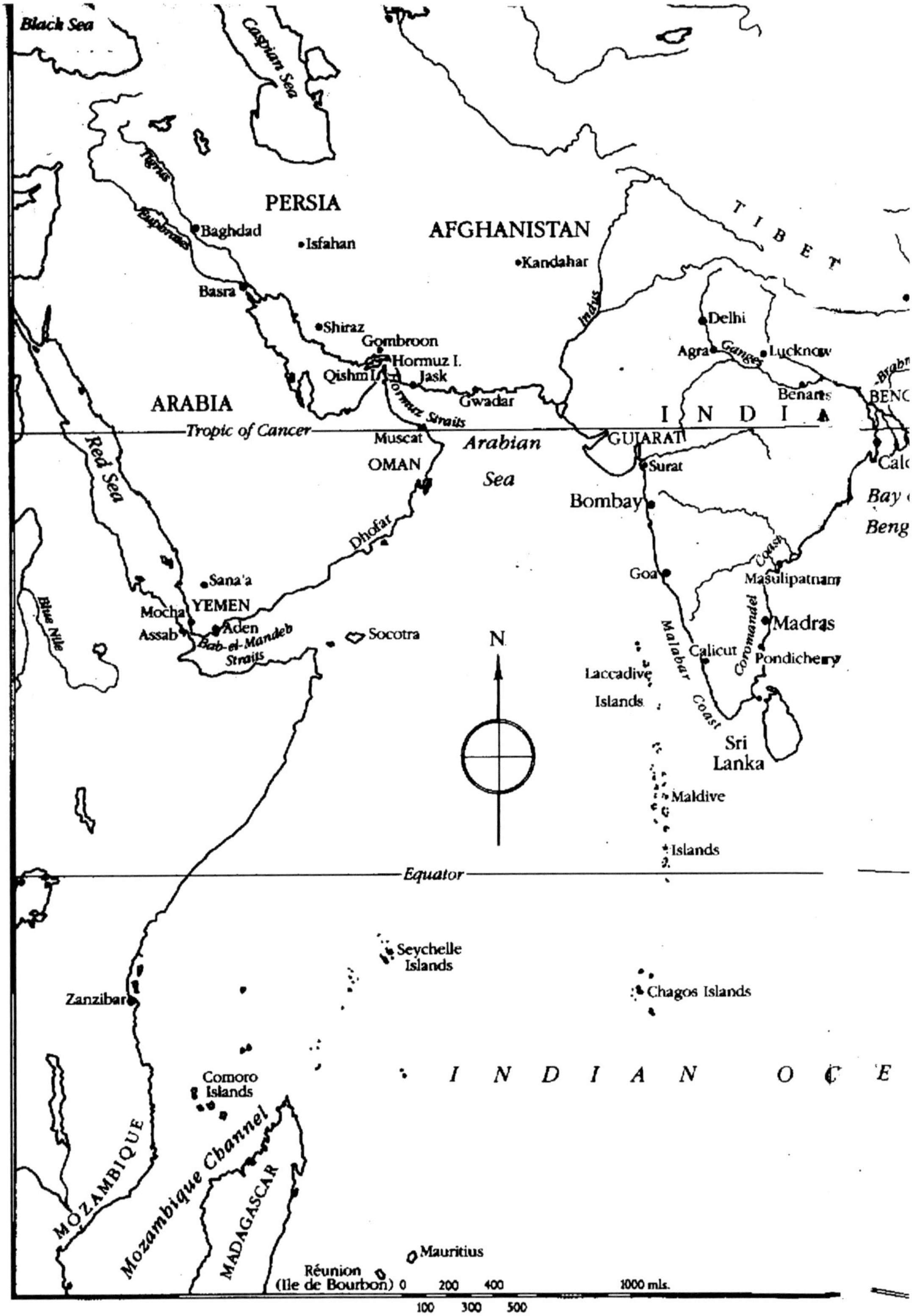
Black Sea
Caspian Sea
Tigris
Euphrates
PERSIA
Baghdad
Isfahan
AFGHANISTAN
Kandahar
TIBET
Basra
Indus
Delhi
Shiraz
Gombroon
Hormuz I.
Qishm I.
Jask
Agra
Ganges
Lucknow
ARABIA
Gwadar
Benares
Hormuz Straits
INDIA
Tropic of Cancer
Muscat
Arabian
Sea
GUJARAT
OMAN
Surat
Red Sea
Bombay
Dhofar
Coast
Goa
Masulipatnam
Sana'a
YEMEN
Mocha
Aden
Assab
Bab-el-Mandeb Straits
Socotra
Blue Nile
N
Malabar Coast
Coromandel
Madras
Calicut
Pondichery
Laccadive Islands
Sri Lanka
Maldive Islands
Equator
Seychelle Islands
Chagos Islands
Zanzibar
INDIAN OCE
Comoro Islands
MOZAMBIQUE
Mozambique Channel
MADAGASCAR
Mauritius
Réunion (Ile de Bourbon)
0 200 400 1000 mls.
100 300 500

Hokkaido
JAPAN
Honshu
Tokyo
Osaka
Peking
Tientsin
CHINA
KOREA
Yellow River
Fukuoka
Hirado
Nagasaki
Kyushu
Yangtze Kiang
Lhasa
Salween
Lucknow
Brahmaputra
Okinawa
Pearl River
Benares
BENGAL
Canton
Formosa
(Taiwan)
Tropic of Cancer
Mandalay
Hong
Kong
TONGKING
Calcutta
BURMA
Bay of
Bengal
Chieng Mai
Hainan
Rangoon
Mekong
ANNAM
Luzon
PHILIPPINES
SIAM
(THAILAND)
Ayuthia
Manila
Madras
CAMBODIA
Mergui
COCHIN CHINA
Pondicherry
Marianas
Islands
Nicobar Is.
South
China
Sea
Balambangan
Island
Pelew Is.
(Palau)
Aceh
Mindanao
Malacca
Singapore
BORNEO
Equator
SUMATRA
Sulawesi
Molucca Is.
(Spice Islands)
New
Guinea
Benkulen
Ambon
Banda Is.
Makassar
Bantam
INDONESIA
Krakatoa
Batavia
JAVA
Timor
OCEAN
Cocos Islands
NEW HOLLAND
(AUSTRALIA)

East India House 1817 .
India Office Records

Introduction

On the last day of December 1600 'the Company of merchants of London trading into the East Indies' received their Charter of incorporation from Queen Elizabeth I. Portugal had dominated the trade routes of the East since 1500, and now Spain and Portugal were one. The sea power of Spain had been broken with the Armada in 1588. The Dutch had been quick to realise this when they sent their first fleet to the Far East in 1595. Now that there was no hope of peace with Spain, the English followed suit. The first voyage was fitted out in 1601. Thus began the Honourable East India Company and the sequence of events which eventually led to the creation of an Indian Empire.

However, this is not the story of the Honourable East India Company, about which much has already been written, although it has to do with the East India Co, and in particular with one of their more humble servants. It is the story of a remote outpost of empire in the 1820s, told by a young Eurasian in the long letters home to his father in England. William Grant Day was educated in England and then sent back to Sumatra with his brother, Tom, to look after his father's spice plantation. In his letters home William writes of the day to day life in the fever ridden settlement of the Company's station at Fort Marlborough (Bencoolen); of the slaves working the plantation; of the opium trade; of the bickering and morals in the small European community; of death and disease and duelling; of Sir Stamford Raffles, the founder of Singapore; of loneliness and boredom and Dutch intolerance; and through it all the insecurity of life and the humdrum business of running a spice plantation. Perhaps also we can read between the lines a little and feel what it must have been like to have been an educated Eurasian in an outpost of Empire.

William Grant Day was born on 10th November 1804 in Sumatra. His brother, Thomas Skottowe, was born the year before. They were the natural children of Charles Day by a Malay mother, Incie Janin. Charles himself was descended from a line of East India Company officials. His father, Thomas Day, had served in India before him and his grandfather, Robert, had served in the Company's home service. Earlier Days still had made a name for themselves in the Company's employ. It is worth dwelling on the history of this East India Co family to help illuminate the background to Thomas and William's letters.

The 17th Century - Francis Day, founder of Madras

The first Day of any note to be mentioned in the East India Co records was a certain Francis Day who joined the Company as a Factor or merchant in 1632. Francis is worthy of note because he was responsible in 1639 for the founding of Fort St. George, later to become the city of Madras (modern Chennai). Although the Company had had its headquarters at Surat on the west coast since 1612, Madras represented the first territorial acquisition of the Company, and certainly the first settlement of any note on the east coast; thus it can be said in no small way to have helped build the foundation of the Company's fortunes in India.

What sort of a man was this Francis Day? My researches[1] have shown that he was the fourth son of William Day of Ockwells Manor, Bray in Berkshire and Helen Wentworth his wife, the daughter of Paul Wentworth, the well known Elizabethan Parliamentarian. Perhaps Francis Day owed his entry into the Company to influence. His grandfather, Dr. William Day, an Eton and King's man, had been a favourite of Queen Elizabeth, which no doubt accounted for his being appointed a Canon of St George's Chapel Windsor, Provost of Eton and later Bishop of Winchester. William's elder brother, George Day, had preceded him at Cambridge and had been made Bishop of Chichester. These two were half brothers, the sons of Richard Daye of Newport, Shropshire who in turn was the son of Nicholas Daye of Wrockwardine, son of John Daye alias Dee, son of Morgan Dee, a Welshman.

It was a foregone conclusion that Francis would be educated at Eton College as his father and brothers before him. His father, William Day, in his will dated 1628 leaves him £200 and expresses the wish that his widow pays him £10 pa. Francis became a cloth worker and in 1630 married Elizabeth Matson, daughter of his deceased near neighbour, Robert Matson, yeoman of Satwell, Berks, by licence at the church of Chelsea, Middx. At the time he and his bride were living in the parish of St James Garlickhithe, London and he is described as about 24 and his bride as about 21.

Perhaps his choice of cloth worker was on good advice, because on joining the East India Company in 1632 he was able to use his acquired skills to advantage. His first assignment was at Armagon, a small station on the Coromandel coast to the north of what was to become Madras. For this he was paid £30 pa rising by £5 pa for seven years. The Coromandel coast was important to the European trading companies because it was here that they could purchase Indian textiles, notably chintz, a kind of painted cloth made nowhere else and highly sought after in Europe. Diamonds, commonly used as a means of remitting money to Europe, were also available from nearby Golconda. Armagon cannot have been a very thriving station because in 1636, in a letter to the President and Council at Bantam in Java, to which the Coromondel Coast was then subordinate, he is described as, "having much improved his knowledge in Armagon goods. We doubt not but Francis Day's care and experience will daily add to the Company's benefit and raise the walls of that decaying fort." Again we read early in 1639, "On the Coromondel Coast there is not one able servant left, unless it be Francis Day."

It was the unsatisfactory state of affairs in Armagon that led him to seek a better site for the Company's station. In 1637 he made an exploratory voyage from Masulipatam to Pondicherry, and in 1639 he again sailed south. In July of that year he arrived at the coastal village of Madrasipatam just north of the Portuguese settlement of San Thome. Discovering the area to be a good source of textiles, he negotiated the grant of a plot of coastal land on behalf of the company from Damarla Venkatadri, Raja of Chandragiri, the local ruler, and in February 1640 began building a new fort, later named Fort St George. For this enterprise, which cost £3500, Day took on loans on his own account. Finding the financial burden excessive, in August 1640 he proceeded to Surat to plead his case with the governing council, who freed him of the responsibility and dispatched him to England as his covenanted period of employment had expired. On 22 October 1641, having served the Company for seven years as a factor, he was admitted to the freedom of the Company by service.

Although the area around Madras was good for textiles, it was not exactly the ideal spot to found a settlement. It had an exposed surf swept beach with no natural harbour for shipping and was only a short distance from the Portuguese settlement of San Thome. However, it was rumoured that Francis Day had a 'mistris' at San Thome of whom he was 'so enamoured' that he would do anything to be near her. On such slender pretexts are empires founded!

He was soon back in India again, this time on a salary of £200 pa and bringing with him money to the value of £17,000 and goods belonging to the First General Voyage, together with his son Francis Day Junior, "as his servant, a good writer and accountant, who is entertained at 20s. (£1) per month on condition that Mr Day Senior stands security for his not indulging in private trade and for his returning in the same ship." He also underwrites the voyage himself to the value of £500 but his request for private trade to the value of £100 is refused. Perhaps returning to India at this time was an astute move, as in November 1641 civil unrest broke out in England leading to the start of the Civil War. It is possible that at least one of his brothers, John, supported the Parliamentarians, because he was threatened with the Starre Chamber for ignoring the King's proclamation on private trade and he was subsequently cut out of his father's will.

Francis Day served the Company well. He also looked to his own interests and in the Company's records there are frequent accusations and counter accusations amongst his contemporaries of private trade, drunkenness and high living. In 1645 and again in 1654 he was recorded in the Company's Black Book and fined £500 for private trade, - the Company guarded their monopoly jealously. History does not relate whether the fine was paid because by then he was out of the service. Having made his fortune in the East he settled down at the age of 40 to the life of a country gentleman in his native Berkshire and acquired a large house in Wallingford called Stone Hall, which still exists today. Only once more does he come into the limelight, as Mayor of Wallingford in 1664, before his death in 1673 at the age of 68. This was quite a respectable age in those days by any standard, and especially for someone who had managed to survive the rigours of two voyages to India.

Francis Day junior also joined the East India Company and went out to India as a factor for Bombay and Surat in 1670. He rose to become fourth in the Council at Surat and died at Bombay in 1693.

Francis Day senior set the pattern for succeeding generations of Days, and no doubt his good works on the Company's behalf ensured their easy entry to that coveted service, where men risked an early death for the sake of a quick fortune and early retirement. The Days on the whole were relatively lucky.

The 18th Century

Coming to more recent times we find recorded in the Minutes of the Court of Directors the following entry for the 28th May 1723: "Petition of Robert Day being read praying to be admitted into some of the Offices: Ordered that the Committee of Accounts be desired to examine the Petitioner's qualifications and make a report." Robert Day would then have been fourteen years old. This was the age at which young writers, that is to say young men of reasonable education whom the Company could employ to copy out reports and write up the accounts whilst they learned the business, were taken on. The report on Robert Day must have been favourable because shortly afterwards, along with three other young men, he is "entertained to serve in the Accounts Office for five years without any charge to the Company".

It was the practice in those days after five years apprenticeship to again petition the Court of Directors, this time for a gratuity for one's past service and a salary for the future. Sure enough, we find Robert's petition duly recorded in the Court Minutes, and after a suitable lapse of time for the necessary "examinations and report", the Court's award, - a gratuity of £30, a salary of £30 pa for the first year and £40 pa thereafter".

It is difficult to envisage what £30 pa then would be worth today. Multiplying by a factor of five hundred would give a salary of £15,000 pa which would compare favourably with the starting salary of a 19 year old clerk in industry or commerce today. But it certainly did not represent riches. Robert Clive writing home to his father as a young writer in India about 1745 says, "The Company's allowance is three pounds ten shillings a month, out of which the money paid for servants' wages, washing, candles and many other necessaries belonging to housekeeping together with the dearness and scarcity of provisions makes it as much as ever we can do to live upon that allowance".

But one must consider more than this. By 1728 the East India Company had been established over 100 years. It had grown from a small trading company of merchant adventurers into a powerful commercial organisation accounting for one tenth of the total English revenue.

Stone Hall, Wallingford, Oxon.

Ockwells Manor, Berks, c1450.
Courtesy of Country Life

Fort St George (Madras) c. 1750.
Engraving after van Ryne, India Office Records

For a young man to have been accepted as a servant of the Company must have meant prestige, the hope of prosperity, and the prospect of future security. There can have been few opportunities of employment in those days that could have offered so much. It would compare favourably with the largest commercial undertakings of today.

However, life was not a complete bed of roses. Charles Lamb wrote in 1833 in his essay "The Superannuated Man" of his years of toil in East India House. He worked there in the accounts office for forty years, writing up ledgers from eight or nine o'clock in the morning very often until eight or nine o'clock at night, Monday to Saturday, from the age of 14 until his retirement at age 54. Sunday was a day of rest, apart from having to attend church twice a day. There was a day's holiday at Christmas and Easter and one week off in the summer, when he would go to the country in Hertfordshire. As he writes in his essay, he just had time to get used to the idea of having nothing to do when he was back at work again. He regarded his years spent there as years of drudgery. No doubt, to lighten the day, he would often surreptitiously scribble an essay when the eye of authority was not upon him.

Robert Day was also employed in the Company's Home service all his working life of 44 years, either at their headquarters, East India House, Leadenhall Street in the City or at Botolph Wharf, near the Tower of London. By 1732 he was already becoming settled because in that year we find he is elected by ballot to be Assistant to the Company's Husband; furthermore "Thomas Boone of Lee Place in Kent, Esq., and Mr. Thomas Day of Charter House Square, Sugar Baker, were approved to be security for £2000", - surely a prodigious sum for those days.

Thomas Boone was the younger brother of Charles Boone, who was a Director of the East India Company and had been Governor of Bombay from 1716 to 1722. There is no doubt that to progress in the EICo you needed powerful sponsors. Charles Boone stood surety for a Thomas Day, a cousin of Robert, when he applied to become a Factor for Fort St George in 1734. Prior to this, in 1725, Thomas had married Elizabeth Boone, the natural daughter of Charles Boone. Thomas died in India in September 1735. There is obviously a strong link between the Day and Boone families. Both families go back a long way in the East India Company records and had probably met in earlier generations.

Round about this time Robert must have felt sufficiently established to get married, which he did at the church St. Gregory by St. Paul on 14th April 1734. In his marriage licence and bond he is described as a bachelor and gentleman of the parish of St. Peter-upon-Cornhill, and his wife to be, Elizabeth Glifford, as a spinster of the parish of St Clement Danes. He gives his age as 24 and that of his wife as 'over 21', although from her subsequent death announcement in the Gentleman's Magazine of 1746, she was obviously only 17. In those days you needed parental or guardian's permission to marry under 21, hence no doubt the deception. Robert's younger son Thomas was baptised at the church of St. Andrew Undershaft in 1738, as were a number of his other children. Elizabeth's death announcement in the Gentleman's Magazine states that she died at the age of 29, in childbirth of her eleventh child. Only three of their children survived.

One can only assume that Robert Day managed to avoid the temptations of office or else was sufficiently adroit in any private transactions that he may have carried on to keep his name out of the Company's Black Book, because his next mention in the Court Minutes is not for a further twenty five years. In 1757 we find that, "It is ordered by the Ballot that on account of the ill state of health of Mr. Robert Day, Mr. James Finlay be appointed Joint Husband and Warehouse Keeper with him at Botolph Wharf. However, it is resolved that Mr. Day do continue his present salary of £150 a year as Husband and Warehouse Keeper and in case of his death that the Warehouse be upon the old footing of an Husband and Warehouse Keeper at £150 and an Assistant at £100 per annum".

He must have been suffering from ill health for sometime prior to this because in 1755 he decided to make his will. In this he is described as a "Gentleman" of Mark Lane and orders his Executors to convert his whole estate into ready money and place the money in Government Securities so that the interest can be used for the maintenance and education of his three children until the age of 21 or marriage. In a codicil he adds "As my son Thomas is going a Writer to Bombay I have advanced him the following sums which are to be deducted from his share:

For his passage to India	£42
Sent him out and carried with him	£100
	£142

Possibly an expensive fare to India by today's standards, but then one must remember that the voyage by way of the Company's station at St. Helena and the Dutch station at Table Bay could take anything up to nine months, that is if one did not die of scurvy, shipwreck or fever on the way. A voyage of four months to Bengal was considered a fast passage. By comparison, the tea clippers at their fastest took around 120 days from Canton in China to the Thames estuary. Today we think nothing of travelling to the other side of the world in a few hours, or communicating by satellite telephone in seconds!

Robert lived a further ten years to enjoy his salary of £150 pa, one can only hope in comfortable semi-retirement. He died in October 1767 after 44 years service with the Company and was buried with his wife at the church of All Hallows Steyning, Mark Lane. It is interesting to note that he was very conscious of his status as a 'gentleman', - not a title to be used lightly in those days. Various members of the family still have in their possession pieces of what must have been a very large East India Company dinner service dating from around 1750. This is emblazoned with the arms granted to Bishop William Day in 1582. This dinner service must have been ordered from China by Robert Day and decorated by Chinese artists with the Day arms, as was the custom in those days.

Robert's second son, Thomas, born in 1738 and baptised at the church of St. Andrew Undershaft in the City, joined the Company as a Writer in 1755 at the age of seventeen and soon after went out to India. Living in Mark Lane, close to the Thames, the Customs House and the Tower, he must have often watched the traffic plying on the river. His father, as is apparent from the witnesses to his will, was the confidante of ship's captains, and no doubt Thomas had the opportunity to go aboard some of the large East Indiamen lying in the docks and hear stories of far off lands from first hand. Perhaps it was this, added to the knowledge of his forbears, that fired his imagination and persuaded him to seek his fortune in India.

His first post as a Writer was at Calicut, a small port on the Malabar coast in the south of India, from which lowly position he rises to become a Senior Merchant after ten years. From there he was moved on to Surat, and gradually over the years worked his way up the Governor's council table until he arrived at third from the top. This was the era of Lord Cornwallis' Governor-Generalship when civil and military office were more clearly defined, and even the Prince Regent's influence could not gain him the favour of a post at Benares. In 1791 Thomas returned home to England and retired to Portland Street, "St. Mary le Bone" where he died two years later. His widow, Rebecca, survived him by a further six years.

The 19th Century - Charles Day

And so we come to Charles Day, elder son of Thomas and Rebecca. Charles Day was born on the 15th July, 1772 in India. His brother Thomas was born three years later. Charles' early education was at Merchant Taylor's School, from where he was admitted a gentleman pensioner of Trinity College, Cambridge in 1790. Either the scholastic life did not agree with him or else the family funds were not sufficiently elastic, because by 1792 he was working at the Banking House of Staple and Co. in Cornhill. Here he stayed two years before joining the East India Co. in 1794 as a Writer for Fort Marlborough (Bencoolen), Sumatra.

His petition to the Court of Directors states that he "..... has been educated in writing and accounts and humbly hopes himself qualified to serve your Honours. He therefore humbly prays that your Honours will be pleased to appoint him a Writer on the Fort Marlborough Establishment; and, should he be so fortunate as to succeed, promises to behave himself with the greatest diligence and fidelity and is ready to give such security as your Honours may require".

His subsequent behaviour does not appear to have lived up to these promises because he was later culpable of what could be called 'creative accounting' and was forced to repay money to the Company.

By this time his father was dead, and one fancies that it was the efforts of his widowed mother which obtained him a position with the Company. Fort Marlborough, noted for its unhealthy climate and high death rate, must surely have been the last place that any aspiring employee would voluntarily choose. Unless of course, the prospect of getting rich quickly in the spice trade outweighed all other considerations. Charles's younger brother, Thomas, who later rose to be a Judge in the Company's legal service, joined the Company as a Writer in 1795. Either he was more fortunate than Charles, or else more discriminating, because he was sent to India, ultimately to Bombay and Surat, his birth place, where he remained for the rest of his life until his death in 1814. It is doubtful whether Charles and Thomas ever met again in later life. Thomas married a Miss Martha Wren, daughter of Christopher Wren of Wroxhall, Warwickshire, at Broach on 8th February

1806. They do not appear to have had any children and she died on 5th April 1813 at Bombay. This Christopher Wren was a descendant of the renowned Christopher Wren of architectural fame.

Charles's first assignment was for four years at Allas, a small station to the south of Fort Marlborough. It was here that his two natural sons, Thomas Skottowe and William Grant Day were born; Thomas sometime prior to October 1803 and William on the 10th November 1804. As late as 1800 public opinion did not condemn irregular unions between European and Indian. In India it was an accepted fact even amongst high ranking officers and wealthy Anglo-Indian officials. The resulting children, if sufficiently fair skinned, were often sent to England to be educated, where at one time it was reckoned that one in ten in the schools was coloured, including those from the West Indies. The tragedy was that when they returned to their native country, as the majority did, they were very often unfitted for the life they had to lead. Having received the education of gentlemen they were reduced to the life of clerks. Prospects were small when their fathers left India and deprived them of such influence as they might have counted on.

Soon after this Charles was moved to Fort Marlborough. Fort Marlborough, half way down the western coast of Sumatra, was founded by the British in 1685. During the 17th and 18th centuries the Dutch had a stranglehold on the spice trade, - nutmegs, mace, cloves, pepper and cinnamon. Pepper was particularly important for preserving meat during the winter months. The British were originally allowed to trade from the Dutch station at Bantam in Java. However, the Dutch ejected them from there in 1682 and the British had to find another base in the far east to avoid a Dutch stranglehold on the pepper trade. The result was the founding of Fort Marlborough in 1685.

The first fort was a wooden, insecure structure but later on in 1714 a more solid construction was built on higher ground. Initially a fixed sum was paid to

Early Day Armorial China c. 1750

Sir Stamford Raffles 1817.
Oil painting by G F Joseph ARA,
Copyright National Portrait Gallery, London

the local population for the production of pepper but subsequently half the payment was made in India goods, which led to abuse of the system. By intervening in local disputes the British were able to impose conditions on the local rulers. One very important one, which became the basis of British rule, obliged local rulers to plant so many trees per year on pain of a fine.

The Court of Directors was constantly exhorting the local officials to increase pepper production. Despite incentives, however, the production of pepper failed to cover administrative costs, much to the displeasure of the Madras government, to which Bencoolen was subordinate. This led to ever more repressive measures until in 1719 the Fort was burned and the British fled. When they returned sometime later planting conditions were considerably reduced.

Bencoolen was notorious for its reputation for ill health. At times such Europeans as were left living were either insufficient or incapable of burying the dead. There were few diversions and continual petty feuding took place amongst the ex patriots. Travel into the hinterland was beset with difficulties. Because of the scarcity of European women, liaisons with the local women were frequent. Contrary to the situation that existed in India, however, the Eurasian population at Fort Marlborough became part of official society. They filled many junior posts in the Company and some became fully covenanted servants.

At Bencoolen Charles must have found more congenial company, although there can never have been many Europeans living there at any one time. In such a small community it cannot have been difficult to shine and it was not long before Charles was Cashier at the bank and Assistant to the Commissioner as Cash Keeper, Treasurer and Civil Paymaster all rolled into one. By this time he was venturing out on his own in the spice trade, for which purpose he acquired a small plantation. Almost certainly he was also dealing in opium on the side.

Charles Day remained at Fort Marlborough until 1807 when he was transferred to Madras. No doubt by this time he had amassed a small fortune; certainly he was lucky still to be alive to enjoy it. We must presume that Thomas and William went with their father to Madras because four years later they accompanied him to England on his return. Although Charles returned home to England in 1811, he did not finally leave the service until 1816. Soon after his return home he married Francis Mary Perreau, the young daughter of his E I Co Bencoolen friend, Robert Samuel Perreau and Mary Cooper his wife, at St. James's, Westminster on 18 April 1812.

Charles Day settled in Southampton with his English wife, a home from home for retired East Indian Nabobs. Here he proceeded to have thirteen more children. One of these, Henry William Day born in 1829, joined the Bengal Army as an Ensign in 1849 and died at Dinapore in 1853, - adding to the last generation of Days to serve in the EICo. Thomas and William, his half-brothers, grew up in the family home, Spear Hall, Bevois Hill, (or Bevis Hill, as William calls it). They would have been about ten when they first came to England. Charles Day died at Spear Hall in 1849.

The Perreau Family

Robert Samuel Perreau was descended from an old Huguenot family from Rochelle, which had fled France around the time of the Revocation of the Edict of Nantes in 1685, as a result of which the Protestant religion was outlawed in France. Unfortunately, the family did not fare too well in England either. Robert's father, also Robert, was an apothecary of Golden Square, London and both he and his twin brother, Daniel, were hanged at Tyburn for forgery on 17 January 1776.

The twin brothers had been found guilty of forging promissory notes on the testimony of Daniel's lover, Margaret Caroline Rudd, although the probability is that Robert was innocent. Caroline was able to copy any signature and Daniel's brother, Robert, as a respected businessman, was the perfect 'front'. In the financially expanding society of the 18th century promissory notes were widely used to raise cash. Lenders were anyone from a bank to a rich family friend. This meant that the promissory note system required both honour and trust. Hence forgery, like murder and rape, was considered a serious crime and carried the death penalty.[2] Caroline herself managed to escape the hangman's noose.

Robert Samuel Perreau was appointed a Writer at Fort Marlborough on 24 January 1777 and arrived in Sumatra in February of the following year. After holding several minor posts he was appointed Secretary to the Bencoolen government on 7 November 1800 and eventually rose to become First Assistant to the Resident and Magistrate. He died at Bencoolen on 22 May 1811. William Hickey, the celebrated eighteenth century diarist, who had cause to remember him, wrote of him:[3]

"Robert Samuel Perreau was the eldest son of the unfortunate Robert Perreau who with twin brother Daniel Perreau suffered death at the gallows in London in 1776, having been found guilty on a charge of forgery. Upon that occasion the usual humanity and compassion of the English showed itself very conspicuously in a feeling of compassion for the offspring of the unhappy victims to the offended laws, and the family experienced every degree of commiseration. The above named Robert Samuel, who at the time of his father's and uncle's miserable exit, had just finished his education at Westminster School, was gratuitously appointed by the Board of Directors a writer on their establishment at Bencoolen and he went out in the year 1777. After remaining at Bencoolen for about three years he obtained permission to visit Calcutta, where he established himself as a merchant and agent, and was supposed to be going on successfully until a natural disposition to embark in every sort of speculation led him to engage in the indigo line, in which from a want of sufficient knowledge of the business, or from some unknown disasters, he finally and utterly failed, and became seriously involved."

However, he was again treated with kindness and his debts made up by his friends. Soon after he suddenly absconded for his original position in Bencoolen leaving a multitude of creditors,

" amongst whom I was a sufferer to the amount of more than five hundred pounds...........not a sixpence of which I shall ever receive he having lately died at Bencoolen without leaving any property or at least that I can discover as attachable.......... Being out of the jurisdiction of any Court in which I could attach him, I had only the poor satisfaction of telling him by letter he was a despicable scoundrel, and deserved a halter quite as much if not more than his father and uncle."

Sir Thomas Stamford Raffles and his influence on the Far East

Almost at the same time that Charles Day was starting his career with the E.I.Co., another young man, or rather youth for he was barely fourteen, obtained an "extra-clerkship" with the Company. Thomas Stamford Raffles joined the E.I.Co. in 1795 in rather different circumstances from those normally obtaining. His father, Master of the "Ann" engaged in the West Indian Trade, was deeply in debt, so Raffles was obliged to leave school, and as he put it in later years "enter the busy scenes of public life".

Whether Charles Day, in his service in England or the East ever met Thomas Stamford Raffles is not known. It is very likely that he did, and if not he could not help but have heard of him. In either event, Raffles's life is so intimately tied up with the history of the Far East that no account of the life and times in that quarter is complete without a brief sketch of his career and achievements. It would be fair to say that Raffles was the architect of British influence in the Far East.

From the start Raffles was a prodigious worker and set himself not only to master the intricacies of the Company's business but also to remedy his truncated education by working long hours after work. He mastered the French language and read both French and English classics.

His interest in the animal and vegetable world led him to study all he could in the rapidly expanding field of natural sciences. All the while his mother was struggling to make ends meet to keep Raffles and his sisters. Of these trying times Raffles wrote," I shall never forget the mortification I felt when the penury of my family once induced my mother to complain of my extravagance in burning a candle in my room".

After five years Raffles's industry was rewarded with a permanent post at £100 pa obtained on merit. About this time he was described by a friend as, "a strange wild fellow, insatiable in ambition, though as meek as a maiden". Raffles continued to work hard for a further five years, five historic years during which Napoleon's armies overran Europe. Once again his amazing capacity for hard work impressed the authorities at India House, and he was awarded the post of Assistant Secretary to the Governor and Council at Penang, an island off the Malayan mainland.

The E.I.Co. had acquired Penang, together with Province Wellesley, a coastal strip further south on the mainland, by purchase from the local Sultan in 1786. In 1805 they had decided to make it a regular Presidency with a Governor and Council and so, at the age of twenty four, Raffles found himself appointed Assistant Secretary, a post which commanded a salary of £1500 p.a. What riches this must have seemed to someone who had once been a penniless clerk!

With his usual energy Raffles applied himself to learning Malay on the journey out, which in those days could take up to nine months. Within a very short time of his arrival he could read and write Malay fluently, and rapidly became indispensable to the Governor and his Council. Raffles set himself to learn everything he could about the Malayan Peninsula, and encouraged the people to visit him and talk to him on all occasions. Before long he became Secretary, but shortly afterwards ill health aggravated by over work forced him to take a holiday in Malacca.

Malacca, formerly a Dutch possession, had been seized along with Ceylon and Cape Town in 1806 during the Napoleonic wars. The Dutch had always controlled the Spice Islands, and the route home via Ceylon and Cape Town. Their sphere of influence met the British in the Malayan Peninsula at Penang and Province Wellesley. Previously the only other British station had been Bencoolen on the west coast of Sumatra. When Napoleon's armies occupied Holland, every Dutch possession in the East Indies automatically became a French possession, and therefore a potential threat to British trade and indirectly to Britain herself.

When Raffles arrived at Malacca in 1807 the Directors at India House had already decided to abandon it. He immediately saw the stupidity of this policy. Lying where the Straits were narrowest, Malacca commanded one approach to the China seas. If Britain abandoned it, it would soon be reoccupied by others. Raffles immediately sat down and wrote a lengthy report to the Directors in England detailing the reasons why Malacca should be retained. On the basis of this report the Directors reconsidered their opinion and Raffles was commended.

A copy of Raffles's report found its way to Lord Minto, the then Governor General, in Calcutta. He thoroughly approved of Raffles's assessment of the situation and considered the former decision of the Directors "a most useless piece of gratuitous mischief"! By now only Java remained in Dutch hands. Lord Minto had long set his mind on the capture of Java and saw in Raffles an instrument to this end. The invasion force set sail in June 1811, led by the Governor General himself. By September the Dutch headquarters at Batavia had been occupied, and General Janssens the Dutch Commander capitulated. By some stroke of irony it had been he who had surrendered to the British at the Cape of Good Hope five years previously. Raffles was made Lieutenant Governor of Java and its dependencies.

Spear Hall in 1850.
Courtesy of Mrs Peter Barker (nee Day).

(Overleaf) Page from a typical letter from William Grant Day, 1823.
Southampton Archives

D/D 1/32 3

Botany Bay Plantation
Novr 29th 1823.

My dear Father,

Often have I sat down to write you an account of ~~the most melancholy event that has befallen me~~ [illegible] have thrown a[illegible] the most affectionate of brothers, and you the most affectionate of sons. His apparent illness was a return of his billious attack, attended with no bad symptoms until the day before his death, when he was taken with a violent & alarming determination of blood to the head, which eventually caused an inflammation of the brains, but it may be one consolation for you to know that he died without one pang without a groan. I have written to Simpson to break the melancholy news to you as gently as he can, being aware of the shock that you cannot but sustain from the loss of so good a son for such he really was!!! he was carried off after the short illness of three days, or I may justly say of only fourty eight hours as the two first days were only attended with severe fever and headache; but they were the unexpected forerunners of his untimely end. Poor Tom died on Wednesday the 29th of October at 1/4 before one oclock in the afternoon, a week before his death Mr Drummond just arrived here by the Bonne [illegible] after an illness of two days, since my poor brother, we have lost poor young Halhed, since poor Halhed, we have lost poor old Captain Salmond, all of them snatched away within a month; fancy then my dear Father what our feeling must be, in so small a community; whose turn it may next be God alone knows, the mortality is really intimidating, but

The Dutch had governed Java with the sole object of making profit. The natives were considered merely as one of the factors necessary for this purpose. A Dutch commission appointed to report on Java in 1790 decided, "they could not fix their thoughts upon it without being affected by sentiments of horror and detestation". "Everywhere the natives are disgusted with the Dutch in Java", reported the British Resident at Bencoolen.

With his usual energy Raffles set out to bestow "on a whole nation the freedom which is everywhere the boast of British subjects". Punishment by mutilation and torture was abolished. Britain had ceased her part in the slave trade in 1807; Raffles determined to stamp it out in Java and as a first step set up a register of all slaves. He converted a feudal system of land tenure to individual leaseholds and threw open the trade. In six months he achieved what the Dutch had failed to do in two centuries of rule. All was not plain sailing with the Directors at home, however, and Raffles incurred their displeasure on several counts.

After the general peace in Europe of 1814 all former Dutch colonies apart from Ceylon and the Cape were returned. Raffles's pleas for the retention of Java were ignored. Although the Dutch reverted to some of their old ways in Java, Raffles's work was not completely wasted. He had set a great example in his treatment and education of the natives. Even the Dutch could not entirely ignore the benefits of his reforms.

In his short reign in Java Raffles did more than restore the Government. His passionate interest in the animal and vegetable world and all things Malayan lead him to visit every part of the island, visiting all the old remains and sending home large collections of flora and fauna for the Oriental Museum at India House. He revived the flagging Batavian Society of Arts and Sciences and did all he could to encourage knowledge and learning of the Malayan scene. Before he was relieved of his post by the Directors at home in 1815 his health had again been failing. His wife and children all died in 1814. He determined to return home to England. On his way back he landed at St Helena and met Napoleon, the man whose actions perhaps had indirectly most stimulated Raffles's own career.

Raffles had left England an insignificant clerk. He returned at the age of 30 an ex-Governor, both famous and wealthy by any ordinary standards. Yet his greatest achievements still lay ahead. The English climate and London society soon revived his health and before long he was as active as ever. In a very short time he had written a History of Java and dedicated it to the Prince Regent. For this and his other services to the country he was knighted. Amongst the many people he met during this period was William Wilberforce, who cherished many of the same ideals and remained a life long friend. He also met the aged Warren Hastings, the man who had dominated the Indian scene of an earlier period.

It was not long before Raffles was again sent out East. His differences with India House had been resolved and he was given the post of Lieutenant Governor of Bencoolen, which had been specially elevated from a Residency for this purpose. Before leaving Raffles married for the second time.

When Raffles arrived at Bencoolen in 1817 the settlement was in a very poor state. Neglected during the war and smitten by earthquakes, Raffles wrote of it, "This is without exception the most wretched place I ever beheld. I cannot convey to you an adequate idea of the state of ruin and dilapidation which surrounds me." With his usual energy Raffles set to work initiating reforms and reviving agriculture. He assumed sovereignty of the island of Pulo Niass, then a centre of the slave trade, and set free the slaves, which incurred the displeasure of the Directors. Although Britain had prohibited the transport of slaves in British ships in 1807, this had not stopped the trade in slaves being carried on by the Malays, who continued to import them from the neighbouring islands in their swift 'proas'. The slaves would be captured from small unprotected villages by pirates; sometimes a man might be reduced to slavery by debt, or would gamble his children, his wife and lastly himself into slavery by betting on fighting cocks.

During this time the Dutch were all the time regaining their former supremacy in the Far East. Raffles realised that if the British were not to lose completely all the advantages they had recently gained, it was very necessary to establish a more central trading station. He put these ideas into another report to the new Governor General, the Marquess of Hastings, who directed him to set up establishments at Achin and Rhio provided that the Dutch did not get there first.

In fact the Dutch reached Rhio first but Raffles, through his Malayan studies, knew of another place, the ancient city of Singapura, then a derelict native village on an offshore island. It was the perfect site, a sheltered roadstead and a fine natural harbour commanding the shortest route between Europe and China, particularly for ships calling at Ceylon and India, as they increasingly did after the opening of the Suez Canal. As Raffles wrote, "not only the European but the Indian world also was ignorant of it." Here in 1819 with the consent of the native government Raffles founded his new colony. The Dutch were furious, as also were the Directors and British Government at home, who at that time were trying to maintain friendly relations with Holland. However, protests were one thing, action another. From the very start Singapore, being a free port, began to attract all the trade of the east and very soon eclipsed all its rivals in size and importance. It was not long before the Directors at home began to change their tune.

In June 1819 Raffles returned to Bencoolen to continue his work. Agriculture began to expand and prosper; he started the cultivation of sugar. His house, as always, was open to the natives. He founded a Bible society, free schools for the native children and finally a native school of industry. He enlarged his collections of specimens and made drawings and plans of the island. As in Java, he travelled all over the island. This for Raffles was a happy time. Death, however, was never far away in Bencoolen. In 1821 three of his children by his second marriage died and the surviving daughter was sent to England. His wife was seriously ill and many of his friends died. During this time Thomas Day died. Raffles wrote home to a friend, "This is a most melancholy day. One of my last letters informed you of the death of poor Drummond after a few hours illness; one of the Mr Days died about the same time. Two days ago Mr Halhed was carried off; and I have just received information that my dear and valuable friend Salmond is no more."

In 1824 a bargain was made with the Dutch whereby the British right to Singapore was established, but Bencoolen and all claim to Sumatra was surrendered; in return the Dutch gave up Malacca. Raffles decided to return home but before leaving he paid a final visit to Singapore. During this visit he founded the Singapore Institute where all branches of knowledge were to be taught, but in particular the study of the Malayan and Chinese languages and literature. Raffles sent home an immense collection of oriental books, letters, paintings, musical instruments, stuffed animals and birds of all description, insects and shells. Fate had another stroke of misfortune for him when the best of the collection was lost in a shipwreck at sea and Raffles himself nearly lost his life.

Raffles returned home a sick man. One might have thought that the work of this great man was complete but he had one more gift for posterity; the founding, in conjunction with Sir Humphrey Davy, of the Zoological Society in Regents Park. Raffles was its first President. He died suddenly in 1826 at the age of 45. If he were in need of an epitaph it might perhaps be found in the minutes recorded in 1819 at the founding of the Singapore Institute:

" I trust in God that this institution may be the means of civilising and bettering the conditions of millions. Thus will our stations become not only the centres of commerce and its

luxuries but of refinements and the liberal arts. If commerce brings wealth to our shores, it is the spirit of literature and philanthropy that teaches us how to employ it for the noblest purposes. It is this that has made Britain go forth among nations, strong in her native might, to dispense blessings to all around her. If the time shall come when her Empire shall have passed away, those monuments of her virtue will endure when her triumphs have become an empty name. Let it still be the boast of Britain to write her name in characters of light."

Thomas and William Day

It is against this background that Thomas and William were sent back to Bencoolen to look after their father's spice plantations. They were received on board the REPULSE in England on 5 January 1821 and arrived in Bencoolen on 13 June 1821. REPULSE was a typical East Indiaman of 1334 tons and undertook six voyages to the Far East in the period 1820-30. Thomas was employed as Assistant in the Military Paymaster's Office but unfortunately died soon after their arrival. William obtained a minor post with the Bencoolen administration until the Dutch took over.

That Charles Day was genuinely fond of these two sons, and they of him, there is no doubt. In his letters home William is continually referring to the happy times spent at Bevis Hill. It is probable that Charles Day had intended right from the start to send his two natural children back to Sumatra and had acquired two spice plantations with this in mind, as well as to provide a useful source of additional income. Perhaps too, in the increasing respectability of Victorian society, he was beginning to regret the ever present reminders of his solitary youth, now that he had a young, attractive wife, social position and legitimate family to maintain.

It is obvious from William's letters that his father writes less and less. William's last letter is dated 31 May 1828 but does not seem to have arrived in England until March 1829. Charles answered this on 16 April 1829, so this response probably wouldn't have arrived in Bencoolen until September 1829 at the earliest. William died in January 1831, which therefore accounts for the correspondence dying out altogether.

Perhaps also Charles grew tired of William's continual complaints about his miserable existence in Bencoolen and thought it was about time he stood on his own two feet; he might have been worried that William would one day turn up on the doorstep of his Southampton home. In one letter William tells his father, almost apologetically, that he has had a daughter, Ellen, born on 12 February 1824, with a native mother but that there is no way that he would want her to be brought up in Europe. Ellen married a private in the Indian army and died at Bombay on 12 September 1846, aged 22. Whatever the reasons for Charles Day's declining correspondence, at least he had done all he could for his early family by bringing them back to England and giving them, for better or worse, the education of young gentlemen.

The two plantations which Charles Day had acquired whilst out in Sumatra were called Botany Bay and Combong. The smaller plantation, Botany Bay, he gave to William as revealed in William's letters; the larger, Combong, he gave by deed of gift to his eldest legitimate son, Charles Arthur Day of Blechyden Terrace, Southampton, for the sum of ten shillings, although this was probably an empty gesture. It is possible that William acquired it by default.

From the accounts which accompany some of the letters it is difficult to estimate the income which Charles Day might have received from these spice plantations. One letter gives the impression that it could have been £500 pa. in a good year, which in today's money would have the purchasing power of around £35,000 pa[4]. The Dutch took over the colony on 1 March 1825 and William died on 6 January 1831, aged 26. It is not known what happened to the plantations after William died but it is most likely that they were sequestrated by the Dutch authorities.

Perhaps it was the loss of income from the plantations which prompted Charles Day in 1834 to invest his money in the rapidly expanding industry of iron built steamships, a good investment in an era when sail was giving way to steam. This investment was to found the Southampton ship building company of Day Summers & Co which lasted for a hundred years, - but that is another story.

There is no mention of William or any descendants in Charles Day's will. It is almost as if this page of his former life is deliberately torn out. But for a handful of letters preserved almost by chance nothing would be known of his early family.[5]

1 See article entitled "The Origins of Francis Day founder of Fort St George (Madras)" by JT Day from the Genealogists' Magazine, vol 28, No. 7, September 2005 for a detailed description of the researches leading to this conclusion.

2 "The Smart - the true story of Margaret Caroline Rudd and the unfortunate Perreau twins" by Sarah Bakewell, Chatto and Windus 2001, tells the full story.

3 Hickey Memoirs vol 4, pp 324, 449

4 MeasuringWorth.com

5 Now in the keeping of the Southampton Archives.

Day, Perreau and Cooper family

—Daniel Perreau (bp. 1733-1776)
—Robert Perreau (bp. 1733-1776)——Frances Keble Perreau
n. 1758 Henrietta Alice Walter (ABT1733-1809) —Robert Samuel Perreau (1760-1811)—
m. 1786 Mary Cooper (1768-1798)
m. ABT1800 Elizabeth Braham

—George Cooper (ABT1728-ABT1798)——Mary Cooper (1768-1798)—
n. Elizabeth
m. 1786 Robert Samuel Perreau (1760-1811)
—George Cooper (ABT1780-ABT1747)
—Elizabeth Kennedy Cooper (ABT1782-ABT1853
m. ABT1798 Duncan Campbell
—Other Children (11)

—Robert Day (ABT1709-1767)——Thomas Day (bp.1738-ABT1793)—
n. 1734 Elizabeth Glifford (ABT1717-1846)
m. Rebecca (Day) (d. 1798)

trees

Robert Perreau (b. ABT1790)
Eliza Henrietta Perreau (b. ABT1791)
Frances Mary Perreau (ABT1792-1868)
m. 1812 Charles Day (1772-1849)

- Charles Arthur Day (1813-1892)
- Robert Ladbroke Day (bp. 1814-1899)
- Cecilia Frances Day (b. 1816)
- Vaughan Cambell Day (b. 1817)
- George Fiott Day (1819-1876)
- Other children (8)

2–Montague Pereau (b. ABT1806)
2–Marianne Elizabeth Perreau (b. ABT1808)
2–Emma Cooper Perreau (ABT1809-ABT1881)
2–Charles Perreau (b. ABT1810)

see children above

Charles Day (1772-1849)
m. Incie Janin
m. 1812 Frances Mary Perreau (ABT1792-1868)

- William Grant Day (b. 1804)
- Thomas Skottowe Day (ABT1803-1823)
- 2–see children above

Thomas Day (bp. 1775-1814)
m. 1806 Martha Wren (d. 1813)

The Letters

Letter 1

Post Mark. General Post Office, Calcutta, 1823
Post Mark. Liverpool India Ship Letter, Bishop Mark E. 21 Nov. 1823
Endorsed: On business and from Thomas Day dated 28 Feb. 1823

To: Charles Day, Esq., Southampton, Hants.
To the care of Messrs Ladbrooke & Co. Ltd, Cornhill, London. T.S.D Perseverence

Fort Marlbro
28th Feby 1823

My Dear Father,

After having commenced and nearly finished my letter to yours dated 8th ulto, I received your letter per ship landed from England which brought our boots and shoes which are a mite too large. I thought Mr. Simpson[1] would have known our measure. My foot I believe is just the same size as his own, and William's a trifle smaller, but he has been sending them for a man of six feet odd. I shall now begin our business. We have received your letters several one dated on your birthday the 15th July 1822 and a second the 12 August 1822[2]. We also received one from Simpson dated the 23rd August 1822 with a list of the things you have been so fatherly and kind as to send for which we feel grateful. He gives us no News at all, he mentions in his letter of having written three letters to each of us. I am sorry to say we have not received one of them. I don't know how he has sent them whether by the way of Bengal or by the ships direct to Bencoolen but we have never received them.

1st, the Plate has all arrived safe from Mr. S. Lamprimondage's and the spoons and forks have all our Initials on them each separately and we have both an equal quantity each, 6 large forks and 6 smaller, 6 large table spoons and 6 small, and 6 tea spoons, 1 soup ladle, 1 gravy spoon, 1 Sauce ladle, 1 sugar spoon and 2 salt spoons. You know I presume by this time we no longer live together for as my brother has entered into the Sugar Concern at Benturin which you must know well for old Perreau[3] had something to do with it, he lived out there with Mrs. R. Winter, which is about twenty minutes ride from my caboon[4]. I nearly every Sunday go to pay him a Visit. I am you know like Jack in the Office, go out into the country on Sunday to pass an idle day. There's plenty of good snipe shooting at Benturin, it being so low and swampy. I have become an excellent shot, for snipes are not the easiest of birds to kill. I now manage to kill three or four brace of them for one day's sport, which I flatter myself is reckoned pretty well. My little gun is very much liked and is just adapted for the Sport.

I will not begin to spin out a long letter to you on my brother William's speculation in the Sugar Concern at Benturin because you will have heard perhaps sufficient from him and Bogle[5] on the subject. It was Sir Stamford[6] and Bogle's doings. Sir Stamford himself promised to write to you also on the same subject. He has given William a situation in the Secretary's office at fifty dollars[7] a month but that is a sinecure berth for he never attends, and here I attend regularly daily and only receive forty dollars a month, but Bogle at first promised to get my salary increased or made up to sixty, but he like a very Jealous fellow, has never put his promise into execution. I cannot mention one kind action your friend Mr. Bogle has done for us since we have been here, he has never once made us a trifling present, not in the slightest way whatsoever. I did expect something of the sort from him as he had experienced much attention and kindness from you when he first arrived in this country. I thought he would have acted in the same toward us. When we first began to keep house we were destitute of almost everything, not a lamp or scarcely a chair, no more than the two wooden ones we brought out with us and I wrote to him to beg the favour of a chair or two and a lamp with a few spoons. The latter he let us have a few, but nothing more. I think that was very unkind of him. I never wrote to him again to borrow anything more. He promised to let us have some Wine and Beer, two dozen of each, but he has never unto this day sent it to us, notwithstanding I have at times put him in mind of this promise!

Bogle had at the commencement of the New Year given over Charge of the Plantation with the Slaves[8] to me, also with the produce already gathered, which I immediately sold to a Mr. Neish a retail and wholesale Merchant residing here, and received the Cash amounting to One hundred and fifty six Dollars which I keep and make use of it for the improvement of the Plantation as it might require it. You must not expect I shall be able to lay by much money for the first two or three months because the Plantation has been sadly neglected, only been manured twice since it has been in Bogle's charge and never ploughed, so I am doing all that now, and intend soon, as fast as I can possibly do it to have it ploughed, and I think next year it will be producing better. This has been a very bad year, Scarcely any of the Plantations have been producing well, Bogle's own Plantations have been producing very little; it is so universal. I have received the Title deeds from Bogle but as to furniture there is but little, he has bought a piece of ground next to Botany Bay, adjoining it formerly Mr. Delamottes who some time ago died and his property was sold, that is his own, and he is making very great improvements; Bogle was living in Botany House and he made it his town house whenever he came into Marlbro, and yet he never thought of repairing it. I think he should have done it at his own expence, as he made use of the house, but instead of it being a little comfortable when we arrived, we found it a perfect cell and filthy dirty, all tumbling to pieces and leaking in every part of the house.

Of Slaves there are few in number on the Plantation, of Men there are four, one almost too feeble and old to work not including two slavemen Bogle gave to wait on us on our Arrival. Three women, two feeble and old, scarcely able to work, one little Boy and, two little Girls, not including two little Boys we have to attend us, which makes ten people on the Plantation, Men, Women and Children, including the old Slaves not able to work, at least very little.

You mention in your long letter dated 15th July 1822 about my writing to Mr. Prince[9] about other horses from Nattal. I really don't recollect having in any of my Letters intimated the subject to you. I might have done so! I did write to Mr. Prince about eight or ten months back to send us two Naga, which he has been kind enough to send us down, and for which I have out of my savings of my little salary honestly paid him the cost. I never in the slightest way ever thought of making you pay again for another Horse each for us, because in this case I was aware you only intended to give us one each, and as Bogle on our Arrival had bought us a couple I could not have wished in any ungenerous and ungrateful way to have tricked you out of another each; and I am extremely sorry you could have ever thought I would ever wish to serve you any such ungentlemanly and dirty trick. I hope you will always find in me a grateful and dutiful and affectionate Son, ever deserving a father's protection and assistance.

I should really be thankful to you for all your small cast off and old Breeches for riding in this Country, and more particularly as we have races, so called, the Marlbro Races which is to take place for the first meeting on the 26th instant and also again on the 27th and as I have always been a little bit of a Jockey I have entered myself as one, so you see that I am not over nice, and will be very grateful for all your old riding Breeches they will fit me I know with the exception of a little alteration round the waist. I have written to Simpson, as a particular favour, for a Pair of Top Boots, a Whip and a good and proper pair of racing spurs to be sent out by the first opportunity. Our races are always to take place twice a year. You may if you please, when you are putting up anything for us also send me two penny worth of Whipcord as we cannot get a piece in this place for any money. We have received all the newspapers, and find them very interesting. I am glad to find you are becoming so gay at Southampton, wish I was with you again to enjoy the Races. Our race ground is near Mount Etchcomb a little beyond Mount Felix.

I should be very happy at any time now to commence to trade in any way you might think beneficial, in Opium[10] I would be happy it is better to begin by times. I would rather at first commencement, your Agents / Fairlie & Co., would send me a few chests of Opium on Commission, on there own Account to sell for them, and let me derive at first some small commission and then after having got a little experience I would launch out on my own Account then should I not think Bencoolen so good a place for the Opium trade as any thing that might be pointed out to me, I would try my better fortune elsewhere. This is now not the place for the opium trade that it formerly was some ten or twelve years back. I only wish those golden days would come to pass again in my time here.

I am extremely obliged to you for the Coblers awls, they are of very great Service. I always have my own Boots, shoes and Sadlery mended at home for I have found one of my own Slaves given to me, is an excellent Cobler, Trim is his Name, he must have been very small indeed when you left this and knew him he was one of your little stable boys. Baskett[11] has been telling fibs we are not near as tall as he asserts. I am only five feet eight inches at present, and I only require my clothes, particularly my coats to be near two moderate sizes larger than my last Coats made in England by Dymott. My Blue coat got so small for me that I was forced to barter with James Grant for a New Europe Coat just imported, for it, as mine was still good and fitted him uncommonly well. My feet are much about the same size that they were when you saw them last.

I am glad to hear the Boys are making such rapid progress I should like to get a Short Letter from them. I think they might be able to write me one with a little of their Master's assistance. Mr. William Lewis[12] a fortnight ago lost his wife and has left behind a young family. He is very much affected indeed, he was dotingly fond of her, she was a Miss Lancaster here, sister to Doctor Lancaster our Assistant Surgeon who died here also some months back.

I now must conclude this long letter as I cannot find any thing more at present to put into it. Tell Miss Perreau[13] I have received her very long letter and am sorry I have not time to answer it but will most certainly have that pleasure by the return of the Borneo who is not yet arrived here. Give my best love and Kindest regards to Mrs. Day and Miss Perreau and accept the same yourself with kisses to my little Brothers and sister[14] and ever believe me to remain

Your affectionate and Dutiful Son,

Thos. S. Day.

Letter 2

From William Day, Bencoolen dated 29 Nov. 1823.
Received May 1824.

Botany Bay Plantation,
29 Nov. 1823.

My Dear Father,

Often have I sat down to write you an account of the most melancholy event that has befallen me here, and as often have thrown aside my pen, Oh, my dear Sir, I have lost the most affectionate of brothers and you the most affectionate son. His apparent illness[15] was a return of his billious attack, attended with no bad symptons until the day before his death, when he was taken with a violent delirium and determination of blood to the head, which eventually caused an inflamation of the brain, but it may be one consolation for you to know that he died without one pang without a groan. I have written to Simpson to break the melancholy news to you as gently as he can, being aware of the shock that you cannot but sustain from the loss of so good a son for such he really was; he was carried off after the short illness of three days, or I may justly say of only four & twenty hours as the two first days were only attended with severe fever and headache, but they were the unexpected forerunners of his untimely end.

Poor Tom died on Wednesday the 29th of October at a quarter before one o'clock in the afternoon; a week before his death Mr. Drummond, just arrived here by the Borneo, died after an illness of two days, since my poor brother, we have lost poor young Halhed, and since poor Halhed, we have lost poor old Captain Salmond, all of them snatched away within a month; fancy then my dear Father what our feelings here must be, in so small a community whose turn it may next be God alone knows, the mortality is really intimidating, but these are not the whole of our list, we have also lost young Anderson whose father I believe you are acquainted with, and my poor brother's former master, Mr. Lewis is also gone to his long home, which makes our number just to half a dozen, since I last wrote you. But I am wavering from the painful subject of my letter, therefore, to return to it.

I shall relate to you the particulars of his death since the sad task is left to me, for not a single soul was with him at his death, but myself and a native Doctor, my poor brother not wishing any other persons to be with him. On the Saturday previous to his death I came to town to attend my office, my poor brother then for the first time complained of indisposition, but notwithstanding accompanied me there; at about 2 o'clock he sent for me to drive him home, being laid up with a fever at Mr. Pattullo's; I took him home, and advised his taking a dose of Salts, which he immediately did, after which I returned to the Country, and did not see him until Monday morning when he complained of intense headache and fever and expressed a wish to see the Doctor, whom I saw at the Governer's breakfast, immediately after breakfast, we both went to see him, the Doctor's opinion was that he would have a return of his fever, and prescribed accordingly, my brother finding himself better towards the evening I did not think it necessary to stop with him, I therefore went into the country.

The following day Tuesday, I wrote him enquiring after his health, an answer to which I did not receive until very late the same night and was surprised at the wild and melancholy style of his note, but the badness of the night prevented my immediately going to see him, but went there the next morning, Wednesday, and found Doctor Stevenson with him; on my entering his room, poor Tom, I perceived was very dangerously ill, he got up from the sofa, threw himself into my arms, embracing me and calling me by my name, until he fainted from the exertions.

The Doctor on my entering the room had left it wishing as he said to avoid the scene he expected to take place, as from the very first he had done nothing but call for me wishing to see me; after fainting he foamed at the mouth upon which I called the Doctor and he desired him to be laid upon the sofa, shortly after, Doctor Bell[16] arrived having been called in by Stevenson, when they advised 20 leeches to be immediately applied to the temples, at the same time giving me strict injunctions to remain with him and keep him perfectly quiet, that they would return and see him again at two in the evening; the leeches arrived at about 12 o'clock at which time he went to the Stool, and from the exertion again fainted and raved, I was quite frightened and sent in for the Doctor, it was with difficulty the leeches were made to bite, for we did not succeed in getting them all on before his death.

About half past 12 o'clock he became more composed, and for the last time spoke of his father and friends at Bevis Hill, his words were "my dear William write my father that I shall soon be better and that I do not forget them all at Bevis Hill" . Shortly after he again went to the Stool and again fainted, but foamed considerably more at the mouth than he had yet done upon which I immediately sent again to the Doctor's, with a note stating the circumstances, upon my turning round I perceived he was anxious to make the people who had entered the room to assist me when he fainted to leave the room, I went to the couch and sat by him, when he said "dear William I feel sleepy". I told the people to leave the room and took a seat by his side, when I took hold of his hand and was looking at him in hopes that a little sleep would do him good, but he shut his eyes to open them no more, nor was I in the least aware of his death until the native Doctor who was putting on the leeches told me of it.

Thus died the best of brothers for such to me he always was, I really did not know the value of a brother until I lost him, but since it has been the will of him who does everything for the best to deprive me of him at a time when I so much required his brotherly advice, I have relinquished him but not without many a Sad tear, never in Bencoolen was any young man so universally regretted by all classes of people as poor Tom was, I had him buried near Mrs. Day's father's tomb.

I must draw my meloncholy letter to a conclusion for at present my spirits are so low that it is with the utmost exertion I have got this far. The next that I write you, will I hope be upon a more pleasing subject, until then believe me to be your affectionate Son,

Wm. G. Day

P.S. Give my most affectionate regards to the ladies and the children, I am fearful of writing Mrs. Day on the subject but I enclose a letter of thanks from poor Tom which he had written a few days previous to his death, it is the last I shall ever be able to send you from him. adieu.

Letter 3

Sent with William's letter of 29th November, 1823

To: Charles Day Esq., Bevis Hill, Southampton Hants,
From: Thos. Day, 1823.

Fort Marlborough
26th October, 1823

My Dear Father,

I hope before you receive this letter you will have received my former ones, my last was dated the 19th July 1823. I am always very particular in sending them in the General Packets for fear they should be neglected for it is generally the case with single letters.

Now to begin. You were anxious before we left you in England to have an Account Current written out by me of the Plantations here, one called Botany Bay, and the Half of Combong. I am aware you wrote to Mr. Bogle concerning that, but I am sorry to say he has never mentioned anything of the sort to me, in fact I am well persuaded he has it not in his power for me to shew me the Account Current of your property here, because the little time I have been here I have been able to see something. The plantation called Botany Bay ought to bring you in clear gain yearly not including the expenses of the Slaves on it, twelve hundred Dollars, which it does make, not withstanding it has been so neglected. Sometimes the Plantation produces seven hundred nuts a day, six and a half, five and four in the bad seasons, some Months it is as low as three hundred and fifty, which it is producing now, but three Weeks ago it was producing seven hundred and six hundred a day. Now calculating that the Plantation brings forth four hundred nuts a day through the whole year, which I think is a very fair calculation - that at the end of the Month is equal to one hundred and twenty Dollars, because the spices now are excessively low, and one hundred nuts with the mace, we calculate, is equal to one Dollar; this is not my own Calculation only, but the old spice Planters, they should know something about them for they are making their fortunes by the spices.

Bogle since we have been here has cut down almost all the Male Nutmeg trees which amounted nearly to two hundred and fifty - there are three hundred and seventeen baring trees in the Plantation, besides thirteen cloves, the chocolate has been all cut down to give room for the female trees for they were so close together that the sun could not get to ripen the fruit. The House is excessively wrotten and Bogle is doing it up a little for us, and in the meantime we are living in Marlborough. To assure you that he cannot know much about the small Plantation, is, that he keeps no account of the spices taken from it, and they are always mixed in with his and sold together, I have no doubt. I do not know if Bogle has ever mentioned to you anything about the Slaves on the Plantation, but they have almost all run away. Some had their freedom given them by Mr. Siddens[17], from the ill treatment of Bogle to them, particularly to the young Women, there is one now here in Marlboro' whom he treated so infamously that she was freed by Mr. Siddens, she has been several times to pay her respects to us and wishes very much to come to us, but she is now a Debtor.

Bogle has been playing the Devil with the people on the Plantation. I'd not like to interfere about anything that he has the charge off - for fear of being on bad terms with him, because he is a very passionate hot Man - and takes offence at the least thing, therefore the best plan is to take things easily until it is our own. You told Bogle to look for a plantation for one of us near about the size of Botany, I fear he will not be able to find one, he might by Chance, if he chooses to exert himself. They are all thinking of making them, not selling them without they are good for nothing. Combong plantation is producing two thousands nuts a Day, sometimes less and sometimes more - he told me he never deducted for the work of his slaves on the Combong plantation, that you had the half of the produce clear. I don't know how far that may be true. He has been remitting money he says to your Agents in Bengal for you a little while before we arrived, he told us he was always remitting money to you. You see it is always the Way, out of sight out of mind. Bogle is getting on uncommonly well he has a fine young Plantation a little way from Combong and another about five miles further in the Country.

Bogle has behaved very civil and kind to us, and we are generally out with him every Saturday evening after Office Hours to stay a day or so. He has not yet made us any present which I expected he would done. He has still got that Buggy you sent him round from Bengal when you were leaving, it has got uncommonly shabby, I thought he might as well now purchase himself a new one and make us a present of that, but he'll drive it much longer yet, he has also a Bay horse you gave him with cropped ears which he also drives now in the Buggy, as he had no idea of making us a present of his old Buggy we have been obliged to buy an old shabby one for the present until we get richer and are able to have one from Bengal. I don't know when that will be, without you take compassion on us! Times are now altered here, there was hardly a Buggy to be seen here and those were without hoods, and now there is not a Common Clerk in any of the offices who do not drive their buggies to office. William has already had an attack of the fever, from exposure to the Sun, but a slight one. We have had many people dying here this last three or four months. Young men not from old age. Sir Stamford has not been able yet to give William a situation in the office. He still attends, but receives no remuneration. Young Grant[18] is also in the same way. Sir Stamford has put them in the Accountants office until there is a vacancy for him.

There's everybody here nearly crying out against Sir Stamford's measures and the way he is going on - except two or three who hold almost all the situations here.

Bob Perreau[19] poor Man I fear will go to the Dogs, he will not take his best Friend's advice. He is every day nearly with Doctor Lucas whom you must know very well and he is making nothing of him. Bogle has been to him and so has all his friends in the settlement. Setting aside all jokes, I really think the man is not in his right senses at times for I have had many instances of his mad fits. You desired us when we left England to send our Measures by every letter to show you how much we had grown, so that, if you were inclined you might send us a Coat to fit us. Now I believe since we left you we have grown about half an inch and stouter, at least I have. I fill out my Coats very well now after living on Rice & Curry every Day. If you should feel inclined to make us a present of a Coat, let them be a size larger each way under the Arms particularly, and do not have the sleeves lined, as it is unnecessary. Brown is not a good colour for hot climates and never looks half as well as blue or black. We are always obliged to wear Mourning here now at the Death of any persons, when attending them to the Funeral and all the Europeans of the Settlement are requested to attend. I have kept my little black coat for that purpose, but I always look like a Hog in Amour in it, for it has got so small. Bob Perreau is just my size, my present coats fit him Dandyishly so you will know his fit now.

It would be a great act of Charity if you could pack up with any things that you are going to send us some Music of any sort, Waltzes, Duets or Piano music - they would be very acceptable. I assure you we are almost always when we do not know what to do with ourselves with a family of the name of Nicholsons whom we find very good and genteel people, when we have plenty of music, and as her Music now has got quite stale so any new ones lately come out would be a rarity, but we leave it to your Generosity. I hope you are all quite well at home, enjoying good Health and Happiness. The children the same. Remember us kindly to all our Friends, about South'ton, the Griffith's, Brooks, etc. etc. and tell the West Coasters what a Hole Bencoolen is now, nothing stirring, no Money to be made, all bearing animosity against each other. William is quite well and unites in love to you all and kisses to the dear little ones, wishing them all Health happiness to see us again some forty years hence when every body has made their fortunes and the remnants for us to pick from.

We are anxious to receive letters from you. I hope you do not wait for the next Stores Ship because you may find plenty other opportunities of sending letters to us by Batavia or by Bengal, you can desire your Agents in Bengal to forward them to us for there are always ships going to Bengal from Europe. If you send them by the Store Ships we shall only receive letters from you once a year - that is a long while to wait. God bless you my dear Father, I wish you Health and Happiness, long life to you to see us once more and believe me to be my Dear Father your most aff. son

Thomas S. Day.

Letter 4

In another hand: From Wm. Day Bencoolen, dated 6 Decr. 1823
Rec'd May 1824

To: Chas Day Esquire, Bevis Hill, Southampton, Hants.

Botany Bay Plantation
December 6 1823

My Dear Father,

I have again taken up my pen for the purpose of making you acquainted with news which I hope will prove more satisfactory than the last, I must however first acknowledge the receit of all your kind letters, 7 in number per Borneo, as also all the clothes etc., sent out by the same opportunity, and other two letters with duplicates per Ship Windsor, under date 10 Jany 1823.

A short time after the receit of the latter mentioned letters I had a little misunderstanding with Mr. Winter my partner regarding an advance made to the concern by Government and not having been acquainted of the same, the advance being (10,000 R's)[20] I thought proper to mention the subject to Mr. W. which caused words to pass between us he immediately got Sir Stamford to grant him fresh title deeds wherein I was deposed of my third share of the dwellinghouse. I was all the time ignorant of what was passing. Two days after poor Tom's death I was surprised to receive a letter from Mr. W. written in a very imperative style, informing me that the avocations of the place did not require my further services and that he wished my things should be moved from the Benturing house as early as possible, after having seen Bogle on the subject, I returned in answer, that it was my intention not to return to the Benturing house, as the late melancholy event had placed me in very different circumstances but I was to be so neutral a person in the concern I should wish to give it up altogether, nevertheless, I wished to know by what authority he could tell me to leave the house as the third share of it was equally as much mine as my other part of the concern, and I referred him to the estimate drawn out by himself wherein the "dwelling house and Coffee Walks (4,000 R's) are included in the 24,000 Rs", but that as it was my wish to leave the concern altogether, it would be of no use disputing the point, would he therefore bring the affair to an accomodation as early as possible, he sent my answer to Sir Stamford, you must first know that one third of the concern belongs to Sir S, and Sir S. is as quite taken aback; however after a few days I had the enclosed paper sent to me for signature and a duplicate of the same was sent to Winter, thus has ended the sugar speculation, and am happy it has turned out not worse than it is, it was on account of your letters that I have thus acted and I hope it will meet with your approbation for I took your letters into very serious consideration as the case will stand very differently as soon as Sir S. leaves this, and no one knows what may be the consequences of a future Residents arrival.

I was almost fearful that I should have lost my situation in the Office but Sir S. has not carried his animosity so far, I am really sorry that I have not been able to meet his wishes as I believe he would have been my friend as long as he was here, but as his reign will so soon terminate I thought it better to leave the concern and forfeit his patronage, I am consequently now living by myself at the plantation, the yearly accounts of which I now forward for your satisfaction, but you must bear in mind that I do not take the credit of having kept them as they are only a copy from poor Tom's accounts, I am happy in saying that the plantation is improving fast, and that the whole of the trees have been manured about three months past and at present I am going to try the good effects of turning up the soil with the plough, as the hoe is too tedious and not equally beneficial, next month I must endeavour to put two more hands on the plantations. I can get convicts at 5 Rs a head per month being the cheapest labour procurable here, for all the people are getting old and infirm for hard work, it would be advisable to emancipate two or three of them, as you will see in the remarks in the yearly accounts, for they receive as much rice and wages as the other people, and it would not be fair to cut their wages after their long services, it would therefore be better to release them and they would be no further burden to the place, where as at present they are a great incumbrance. I shall however wait for your instructions, Bogle has rented Combong at 3,500 Sicca Rupees a year to be paid in bills on Bengal, and he is bound yearly to plant out 200 trees, and it is at his option to throw it up in three years, in failure of either parties not acting up to the agreement, there is attached a penalty of 5,000 Sicca rupees.

Regarding my poor brother's property I should wish you to authorize me to succeed to what little property he has left. I have had permission from Government to become his Executor, and have entered into the usual agreements in similar cases, a copy of my letter and the answer to the same I now forward; as yet I have not sold any single thing as the many recent deaths have completely lowered the market, and things are now selling at 50 percent discount. You will see that I am to "pay into the Government treasury the amount proceeds of the estate, within 12 months from the present date", but I have been informed that it is 12 months from the date of the auction taking place, I shall therefore defer the same as long as I wish, and I shall in the meantime pay off all poor Tom's outstanding debts, what property there is, belonged to us both, you must be aware that as everything was between us, but I do not like to speak to that effect to Sir S. as I am at present not one of the elect, and he might doubt the veracity of my assertion, for he is not scrupulous in such matters, more especially with those who have crossed him in his wishes. I hope then you perfectly see my reasons for writing you on this subject, but bear in mind, I do not assume to succeed to all my brothers property, but I do not think there can be any very great overplus when I have paid the expenses of his funeral and all his outstanding debts, but as I am myself free from debt, I shall be able by degrees to pay off all those against my poor brother.

Bogle has got Combong at present in very fine order and I see he has been planting young trees. I think Baskett has managed very well with regard to renting the plantation to Bogle. Plantations will be very numerous shortly, as by poor Captain Salmonds death we shall have a few for sale, and Baskett has told me that he is commissioned by you to purchase one for me if cheap under the proviso of my giving you a mortgage on the place for the advance of the purchase money. I assure you my dear Sir that at present the spice is the only profitable speculation now going, and I think that in six years any plantation will pay itself, but it is improfitable to begin a young plantation as labour at present is remarkably high, unless interest can be made to get convicts free of expence from the company, and that cannot be done unless you plant coffee for it is under these conditions that individuals are allowed them, but a plantation in bearing with spare ground to keep gradually increasing it is as profitable a speculation as any in Bencoolen, and be assured that should Mr. B. purchase a plantation for me, that I shall not be wanting in my part to pay every attention to it.

I think I can say with every propriety that I am in every respect much changed for the better since my arrival in India, for I am no longer the negligent boy I was when in England for I have found out that if I do not take care of myself no one else will for me, and still more so since I have lost poor Tom, when he was alive I really had a friend but now I am destitute of any one in whom I can place real confidence, as to Mr. Basket he is a man in whom no one can place any kind of friendship for those who do are ruined men, as they are sure to be immediately involved in his books, his friendship consists in lending money at most exorbitant interest, I therefore have always avoided having anything to do with him, for it is under the cloak of friendship that he has ensnared the greater part of the young men here, as yet I am happy in saying that I have avoided getting into his black book. As to Bogle he is a man who courts no ones friendship and keeps very much to himself, and of the two I would certainly prefer Bogle, so you see how I am situated.

Baskett has promised to write to your agents to send me down five chests of opium according to your instructions, I am only sorry I could not have got it down this year, for when the Eastern boats were here, we had not a single chest for them, and were obliged to send to Peking for it, what a handsome thing I could have made by it, but I hope to try my luck next year, and be assured that I shall not appropriate the money realized by the opium for any other purpose but for opium solely, as I always bear strongly in mind the promise of visiting old England after having been in India for ten years, and hope in that time to be able to do so, just to take a peep and off again for it is really heartbreaking to think that we may not see our friends again in this world, and without hope life would be unendurable.

I have sent you my poor brother's watch and his seal that has his crest upon it, but the one with his name engraved in persian characters I have kept myself, his watch key I gave to Bogle, and his new coat that you last sent out I gave to Robert Perreau. I also send in the same box, my poor brother's sleeve buttons which are for Miss Perreau, also an ivory card case, which poor Tom had made purposely for Mrs. Day and two locks of his hair, one of which I send to be set in a ring for myself, whatever the expence may be I shall feel happy to defray it.

You have been kind enough to order to be sent to us two pipes of Cape Maderia wine, as yet it has not arrived, but I hope it is forthcoming. Your kindness has been so great that I do not hope to return it, nor when it will be in my power to do so, and be assured that I shall never forget it, I hope shortly to be no longer a burthen to you, as I shall discontinue drawing upon you for the fifty dollars a month as soon as I can get an increase of salary, as I really cannot manage with less than 75 Dcs. a month considering the appearance I am obliged to keep up for those with whom I am in the habits of associating with, not one of them draw less than 5 or 600 Rs. a month and I am obliged to cope with them on 200 Rs. a month or forfeit their Society for that of the other office lads in the place, as I am the only exception of a monthly writer being admitted into the society of the Civilians, it is only within this last twelve months that I have been admitted to their parties, and I have now got myself upon a most friendly footing with all the Bachelor Civilians in the place, as the married people keep themselves very distinct, only inviting the bachelors now and then to a formal party, of which I am generally one of the number.

My paper is drawing very fast to a close therefore allow me to conclude with wishing you all the compliments of the season with love and regard to you all, and kisses innumerable to my little brothers and my sister Emma, I remain your most dutiful and attached son,

Wm. G. Day,

P.S. Give my best love to John Edwards, I shall not write him as he begrudges the postage[21].

Included with letter from William Day dated December 6 1823.

Endorsed: To Chas. Day, Esquire, Bevis Hill, Southampton, Hants

To Chas. Halhed Esquire
Secretary to Government

Sir,

I have the honor to acquaint you for the information of the Honble the Lt. Governor that my late brother Thomas Day has died intestate and having no one here nearer related to him than myself it is my wish that I may be allowed to administer to the estate provided I can obtain the sanction of Government for so doing. I should therefore feel much obliged by your submitting my letter for the kind consideration of the Hon'able the Lieutenant Governor.

I have the honor to be
Sir
Your Most obedient Servant

Fort Marlbro.
5th Novr. 1823
A true copy.

Wm. G. Day.

To W.G. Day Esquire

Sir,

I am directed to inform you that you are authorized to administer to the estate of your late brother Thomas Day under the following regulations. That you enter into a security bond for the due administration of the said estate, and for duly paying into the Government Treasury the amount proceeds of the estate, within 12 months from the present date, according to the true and particular Inventory of the same, to be recorded in the Pangerams[22] Courts.

I am
Sir
Your most obedient Servant

Fort Marlbro
6th Novr. 1823 Chas Halhead
Wm. G. Day. Registrar
A true Copy

The agreement subsisting between Richard Winter and William Day both of Fort Marlbro as per Deed under date 27 Day of August 1822 is this 8 day of Novr. 1823 by mutual consent of the parties cancelled, and all contracts and agreements entered into between the said parties are hereby consequently dissolved. All the demands and claims against the Sugar works called Stamford Lodge are to be adjusted by Richard Winter from which demands and claims in whole or part the said William Day is entirely exonerated, He having hereby transferred and given up to the said Richard Winter and by these presents do transfer and give up to the said Richard Winter all claims title and right to or in the said Sugar Plantation called 'Benturin' or to or in any part or parts thereof. In witness whereof the parties have the 5th day of Novr. 1823 set their hand and seals.

Witness
Robert Bogle — Signed R. Winter
Pat Neish — Wm. G Day
A true Copy.

Letter 5

On cover: From W. Day dated 24 Decr.1824

Bencoolen
24th Decr. 1824

My Dear Father,

Your long expected letter, respecting the transfer of this settlement to the Dutch, has at last come to hand; accounts reached us three months back via Batavia, of such a circumstance being about to take place, since which time we have had no other accounts than those by this opportunity; at one time we had our doubts as to the truth of the report, from not having received any official accounts respecting it, but to our sorrow we find it too true! News so truly distressing came upon us like a thunderbolt. I have been obliged to muster all my philosphy to enable me to bear up with it, and have hardly yet reconciled myself to it. Only think how many of us will be thrown destitute in the world by these unprecedented acts, something on the subject might have been intimated to us but to carry on the business in so clandestine a manner was really shameful! but enough of this, as what I say on the subject can in no way avert the impending blow.

Your letter to me was far from being unkind, on the contrary, it would have been more so had you not written to me as you have done; I had nevertheless long before made up my mind on the subject: in India I had determined to earn my bread, and never to make myself a burthen to my friends, from whom I have received more attentions than I was ever entitled to expect, let your mind, my dear father, rest at ease on this point, even had you invited me home, I should have been reluctant to have accepted of it, otherwise than my assurance of your good wishes for my welfare had dictated you to make such a proposition, nothing else would have induced me, and by the same feelings I am at present actuated. As to my leaving Bencoolen for Malacca or elsewhere, it would be folly in me to do so; here I have a house with as many comforts as most young men in India, I mean not domestic ones as they are not to be found in this quarter of the Globe. But what I mostly regret, is the death of my poor brother Tom, the meloncholy particulars of which you must have learnt ere this: by living together we might have managed to make both ends meet. I only hope to have the good fortune to get a gentleman fellow for a chum, to share my monthly expences; as I cannot expect to get employment until such time as I am proficient in the Dutch language, consequently a Dutch companion will greatly facilitate the attainment of so material a point. I hope I shall not incur your displeasure if I continue to draw upon you for the same amount as I have hitherto done, at the rate of 50 R's (fifty) a month. If out of employ / of which there is not a doubt / how shall I subsist? but when other means turn up I shall then immediately discontinue the same, knowing too well your inability to afford any such supply.

I shall not fail to take the necessary precaution of having the Title Deeds of Botany Bay Plantation registered in the Magistrates office and attested by the authorities here; the Dutch character is too well known at Bencoolen, the acts of their Government at Batavia & Padang speak for themselves. A more arbitrary nation there cannot be - pleasant prospects for a poor man, but it is to be hoped that it is all for the best! As to poor Robert what will become of him, God alone knows! he is becoming daily worse and worse, I am fearful past all redemption. I write you candidly my opinion and the opinion of every one here; his poor aunt writes in such an affectionate manner respecting him that I should hardly wish her to know the contents of this paragraph of my letter. If the ladies see it I hope they will not think me unkind for writing what I have done; both of them make anxious enquiries in their letters per last Indiaman / which letters I propose answering in due time / whether his illness was brought on only by drinking. I am fearful it was so! He has lately purchased a house without my knowledge or even consulting me on the business for a sum far exceeding its value. I am not even informed of the terms upon which he has purchased it, he avoids my company as much as possible, he is probably aware that I give too true a character of him to his friends at home, I can assign no other reason for his extraordinary line of conduct. [*The whole of this paragraph was crossed through and marked Robert P*]

It is a lucky hit that matters were settled between you and Bogle respecting Combong, he is wishing to be off his agreement, but do not mind his soft words; he has made too good a thing of that plantation for the last fifteen years, it is now your turn to reap some profits from it, I perceive he has been planting out in fulfilment of his agreement - again I say by no means listen to his proposals, the plantation is in very good order, much better than before! I was on the point of purchasing a plantation when the news of the transfer arrived, a few days longer consideration would have made it mine. In the mean I shall give up all idea on the subject until such time as I see how things turn up. You may depend upon my taking no steps without consulting Baskett on the business. As things have turned out I was also very fortunate in getting rid of the Sugar Concern at Benturing, the agricultural interests of Bencoolen have certainly received a severe shock. Bogle does not know what to do, perhaps he thinks it a judgement upon him for past offences!

I wrote to your agents in Calcutta, upon the strength of Mr. Baskett's recommendation for 5 /five/ chests of opium on his own account by the same conveyance - Previous to closing my letter I showed the contents to Mr. B. who approved of the letter and enclosed it with his own particular recommendation to them. So says Baskett! to ascertain the truth of which I intend addressing the house another letter on the subject - as I have my doubts whether the letter was ever sent. Had I received the opium at the time expected I should have sold it exceedingly well but I firmly believe was never sent, as two opportunities have offered since even the arrival of Mr. B's opium before alluded to, Baskett, Bogle & Lewis have every year monopolysed the opium, and my letter has been retained to prevent my spoiling their market. I have almost learnt that the word "friendship" is not known in trade! Such circumstances as these are not uncommon in Bencoolen. This is not the first slippery trick Baskett has played me, twice he disappointed me respecting two plantations - but as things have turned up it is all the better for me. One plantation I proposed purchasing he purchased himself notwithstanding he told me that he was negotiating with the proprietor on my account. The second /a very desirable plantation to me for many reasons / he let a Parsee Merchant have; who was indebted a large sum of money to him, immediately after the purchase he made the poor fellow give a mortgage upon the property such are the results of profession of friendship in this quarter of the Globe.

You mention in your letters per Harris, that you "supposed by this time that our wine was drunk out", so far from its being drank out, as yet I have not received it, or had any other accounts of it than by your letters, I think your letters must have miscarried /a not too uncommon circumstance in India / it certainly would have been very acceptable, for at present we pay in Marlbro no less than 30 Madras rupees a dozen for Madeira wine - and all other spirits in like ratio - as to myself I never require them but am obliged to have them for my friends, credit what I tell you when I say that I have as great an aversion to spirits as when I left England this time four years. Bogle seems to be very particular in his reports to you regarding us both. Do not give too much credit to his assertions, I do not recollect ever sending over to his house for "a bottle of brandy". I will defy Bogle or anyone else in the settlement to assert that I have ever been seen in the highest degree intoxicated. It is more than any other man can say of himself in Bencoolen! Endeavour to ascertain from some of your Bencolen correspondents whether such is the case. I know full well the source of your information, notwithstanding you call him a "stranger", but he is no stranger to me.

I did think at one time Bogle had acted a friendly part toward me by getting me with the Benturing concern. But I am no longer of that opinion; as he played me a very sly game when I threw up my share of the concern. When you write to him again on the price of nutmegs say that you learn a different story from me. Good nuts are pr pecul[23] 200 Guilders[24] and not 70 Drs. Ditto mace sold separately 220 guilders and not 80 drs, but if sold together only 200 guilders - a pecul. My last sale of spices were certainly lower than I have ever sold them before, owing to the treasury being open for tenders of money for bills on Bengal, by which you make a sure remittance, where as by spices you make a very uncertain one, this is the reason of the fall in spices - had I waited till now I should have done better - but I was pushed at the time for cash to buy Rice.

Averting to the amours of my poor brother with Mrs. N., I plead his cause by saying that his soul rests where charity forbids reproach! Some people have wished to be very wise on this subject, but none ever dared or could authenticate the scandal then afloat in the settlement. How often poor fellow has he asserted to me upon his honor, that he was innocent. On Mr. N's. return these reports reached his ears - My poor brother was then no more! I felt myself in duty bound to explain everything to Mr. N. with which explanation he was perfectly satisfied. The occasion of Mr. N's. leaving this for Bengal was a quarrel with this Government, and he had gone to headquarters to seek redress, at that time the settlement had "cut him" he had no one but poor Tom to ask to be the friend and companion of his wife during his absence - with a request to give her an airing in his buggy now and then from which circumstances has originated all the scandal regarding poor Tom and Mrs. N.

The story between Mrs. N. & Doctor Bell I believe to be strictly true, he / Dr. B./ took the opportunity when Tom poor fellow! had left this for his health. Tom took every opportunity of letting Dr. B. know his sentiments regarding him, but he was a white feathered gentleman and would not take a hint - but required to be "kicked" before he would call a man out - poor Tom did not go exactly to these extremes with him, but did every thing else but kick him. Ultimately Nicholson called him out, and I stood his second - it was then that Dr. B. show'd his horns. Since which business he has never been able to hold up his head, and if justly treated should never be again admitted - with the Society of gentlemen - but you must know that Dr. B. was Sir Stamford's Body Surgeon. On Sir S's. learning the particulars of Dr. B's. conduct he discarded him from his house and table but to the astonishment of every one he was shortly after reinstated into the good graces of the folks at Government House. The general opinion is that Lady Raffles interceded for him. He has gone home with his family to let this faux pas blow over, but Nicholson will never allow such a such a thing to remain quiet, as he Mr. N. is now situated in Calcutta Dr. B. cannot return there without Mr. N's. knowledge and he Dr. B. will no longer have the Lieutenant Governor to screen him from the attacks of an injured man.

When Dr. B. met Mr. N. for the purpose of affording him every satisfaction that one Gentleman required from another he thought it best plan to let N. take one shot at him and not return N's. fire - tho' the conditions of the meeting were that "one of the parties should fall". Nicholson branded him with the name of villain, rascal, coward, etc. but all would not rouse him to return Mr. N's. fire - so obliged Nicholson to leave the ground as little satisfied as when he came. I have entered thus fully into the business that you may not be misled by misrepresentation of the affair, as Nicholson is man of very respectable connections in England who will not let Dr. B. be perfectly quiet - and as the thing may come to your ears I thought it as well to give you an account of it. I understand gave him a letter to you[26] - after what I have written you cannot give him any countenance for in every sense of the word he is a "Blackguard".

The Melon seeds you sent me turned out very well, I did not plant them myself but gave them to Lieut. Anderson who is something of a botanist, with whom they succeeded very well. They were very good flavoured and much too good to be put into a Curry when common pumkin would do as well - formerly I had a very good garden of my own, but I found that it took one man's entire attention to keep it in any like good order. Nevertheless I have a little flower border in front of the house and any spare flower seeds or seeds of any description will be always most acceptable. The lamps arrived safe, with the exception of one of the shades being broken. They are very handsome and are well adapted for this country - the only fault in them are that the burner's should have been Globe ones - the other ones are more apt to break, but nevertheless accept my most sincere thanks for them as well as the other things you have been so kind as to send me from time to time. Should you ever have again occasion to send a parcel to Bencoolen let me beg of you a small quantity of thread and needles - things tho' of little value are not procurable in Marlbro.

In speaking of the buggy whips Simpson says "hangup whips", all that I know about the business is that I got two whips out of a bundle of whips bought out by Baskett for sale, made expressly for that purpose, those sent by Simpson I have reason to believe he kept for himself, as I have remarked his using a couple of "hang up whips" when he has occasion to go out - whether such is the case I do not know, but I leave you to judge.

As yet I have not written to Montague Perreau[26] knowing his regiment to be engaged in the present Burmah war. I intend doing it the next opportunity that may offer. The accounts from Bermah are very bad, all the troops dying like rotten sheep as yet they have not been able to come to an engagement - it is not known yet how it will terminate, there has been a most serious mutiny in the Bengal Army, no less than 500 sepoys shot while under arms with marching orders. As yet we have not heard the particulars otherwise than the report brought by this ship. If it is actually the case it will be a serious thing.

You must excuse my scribbling at this rate but I have not time to make a fair copy - only think of having sixty seven sheets of a dry Missionary Report upon the Batan Country to draw out in duplicate and triplicate[27] - it is enough to make a fellow sick of the sight of pen, ink and paper.

I am truly glad to hear that my old friend Captain Bullen has got a Command, may he meet with every success is the sincere wish of my heart. Remember me most kindly to Mrs. Bullen - and tell her that her attentions are yet as fresh in my memory as when I left England this time four years - a hobyty hoy - I do not acriefy[28] the old saying out of sight out of mind, on the contrary my heart is too often straying and recalling to mind days of happiness which are past and I fear never again to return.

You will be enquiring into the occasion of my long silence, do not attribute it to want of intention, but actually from want of opportunity. Bencoolen is perfectly deserted and is gradually going out like the snuff of a candle. I do not know whether I shall time to write the ladies a line by this opportunity, but I'dd do my best in due course should they not get one this time. Let them be assured of getting one by the same opportunity as the one when I intend answering your numerous queries. This letter goes via Batavia, Mr. Lewis goes down with the intention of putting his children on board the General Harris for England, consequently this is a quicker channel of communication than the one now at Bencoolen per Larken via Bengal. By the latter opportunity you may expect to hear from me - as yet I have said nothing respecting my brothers and sister - May God bless them and their parents are the earnest prayers of my heart. We drank on Christmas Day "Absent friends". It gave me pang when I looked back upon the meloncholy changes of the last four years, since poor Tom's death I have found a great alteration in my spirits - true friends are not to be procured every day in India - and until the loss of my poor brother I really did not know the value of one - I have now learnt how to estimate one - and when I find I shall do so. With Love and kisses to all at home - and kind remembrances to all old friends, I remain,

Your Affectionate &. Dutiful son,
Wm. G. Day.

P.S. I have been endeavouring to fold up this letter without an envelope and as I find I cannot do it without making a very clumsy concern of it I thought it as well as to fill up this space. I'll give my head another knock and see if I cannot knock something more of it.

What do they think of Sr. Stamfords conduct during his reign in Bencoolen, we are given to understand that a few questions are awaiting in England. Baskett has completely taken a new lease of his life, he now enjoys better health than ever. I forgot to tell you that I had this season a touch of a billious fever which laid me up for about ten days. I however soon managed to shake it off. Jas. Grant has at last settled himself in Bencoolen and entered into a speculation with Baskett by taking a half share of a very large nutmeg plantation, he is likely to do very well. He is a very steady fellow, for the last six months we have been chumming together - but as his house is finished at Woodlands he has gone out to it and I am now again all alone. Remember me to the Griffiths'.

Old Grant, I think, is duty bound to do something for my brothers as he never did anything for me, that you full well know. Old Fiate and his family I also include in my list of remembrances, Minchins, etc., I intend answering Frederick's letter, tell him so. I do not think he half liked my last letter to him, since I have been in India I have not had a line from him. So much for his friendship! Whatever may be his feelings towards me, nevertheless tell him I sincerely wish him well, and that I often revert to moments past together at Dr.Iwing's.

I forget to mention that I have become a bit of a proficient in the violin. Again adieu.

Letter 6

Endorsed: From Wm. Day 18-19 February 1825.
Ship Letter Wight.
Endorsed in pencil: Not to send back the dog Rosa. Wm. to live in Combong house with........If he will not rent it.
To destroy all my letters. Watch Robert is not............

To: Chas. Day, Esquire, Bevis Hill, Southampton,
Hants.
Per Padang.

Bencoolen,
18th February 1825

My Dear Father

A favorable opportunity now offering for England by a Dutch ship bound to touch at Portsmouth and drop a packet I have taken up my pen to let you know that I'm still in the land of the living. I wrote you a long letter about six weeks ago, full of grievances, no others, thank God! have since occurred of which I have to complain of.

As yet we have received no further intelligence respecting this transfer. No Leighton has as yet arrived, I am fearful some accident must have befallen her or something unforeseen has occurred. She ought to have been here the beginning or the middle of last month. I'm in anxious expectations of hearing the tidings. She will bring, we know, nothing further respecting the Dutch than what we can learn by the gazetts, and the printed treaty. It is rumoured that they take possession on the 1st March - but we have no official accounts of it. All we poor writers in the offices expect to be discharged at the end of this month, every preparation is making for the arrival of the Dutch. The ship just arrived from Padang, brings no further news than a report of the Dutchmen not being able to take possession for four or five months, as they are engaged in a very serious war at Macasser - and are also at Palembang, they certainly have enough to do. When they take possession of Bencoolen; and I think they will have some work to keep Sumatra quiet - I do not recollect whether I told you that I have written to Ferguson & Co., for 5 Chests of opium which they did not condescend to answer - I have since learnt from Baskett that they wrote him on the subject; their excuse was not having any authority from you for so doing - had they sent it I should have cleared 800 R's a chest by it - which would have relieved me from all incumbrances previous to drawing up and balancing my accounts on the arrival of the Dutch - It will be an awful day for many of us when it does take place "Apo bouli boit"[29] as we say in Malays. I have made up my mind to put up with the sweets and bitters as they come - with the calmness of a Stoic that is to say if I can.

You may expect to hear from me most fully by the Leighton - This epistle is only to be considered an interlude, as the opportunity was quite unexpected - Riding out the other morning I had the misfortune to loose one of my gold sleeve buttons given me by Miss P. I almost cry'd when I discovered my loss. I have sent the remaining one round to Calcutta to have a fellow one made to it. Rosa is in very good health but getting quite grey from old age - be not surprized if you see her one day sent back to Bevis Hill to finish her days. I often think of Bevis Hill "days of auld lang syne" when I am here. Robert Perreau is in good health but I tell you candidly that he is a lost man - only between ourselves I shall be more explicit in my next, he is growing worse and worse - make my most affectionate regards to the ladies and kisses to the little boys - they must write me how they like school. You have a likeness of my poor brother taken in pencil, may I ask you for it - I should esteem it a particular favour, it was thought a good one at the time it was taken just before he left England. You can easily get it copied, either send me the original or the copy.

What is poor Allen doing, and John Edwards, remember me kindly to them both and to all old friends and servants at Bevis Hill. With every hope I wish for your enjoyment of a good state of health not only on your account but that of your dear family is the constant prayer of your own dutiful and affectionate Son,

Wm. G. Day.

I'm badly off for shoes! My coat is getting rather tight across the shoulders! No hint. Any gloves or watch ribbons would be acceptable to sport amongst the Dutch frows. I have only mentioned these circumstances by way of filling up - leaving it to your discretion to comply with the same

Letter 7

Bencoolen
February 1825

My Dear Father,

I have again resumed my pen to answer your letter dated 25th of June 1824 which has this moment come to hand. You will also receive of this opportunity another letter dated a day later than this, which I had written, but as the ship does not sail till tomorrow morning I will endeavour to get this off, tho' not certain of its being in time; for your letter was brought tonight after having turned into bed - my ideas are at present rather dull - I am happy to hear that my poor brother's trinkets arrived safe to hand. I kept his seal with the arabic caracters, as a memento of my poor brother; but should it be my lot to be carried off, I have already left instructions in my will, to send home my watch, seals etc., to my friends in England with a lock of my hair.

On the death of poor Tom, I was induced to make my Will, I had certainly not left you my Executor, but had left a friend to act solely, however, I shall by the first opportunity send you a copy of it. I can easily make a fresh codicile, and leave you an Executor also - You say that "you presume I will leave every thing I may die possessed of to you and your heirs" I have not exactly left it to you, but have left the whole of my property to my only sister Emma - my brothers can fight their own way through the world, but Emma poor little darling, should anything happen to either you or her mother - she would claim my pittance or protection before her brothers - I hope you will see that I am actuated from the best of motives by acting as I have done, but as you may not at a future period / when I am no more/ be surprized I must make you acquainted of my having a child A Girl now upwards of twelve months old - for whom I have left a subsistence, as well as for the mother.

I have been induced to write you thus candidly, that hereafter you may not tax me with not treating you with the candour that you have ever treated me, but let your mind be under no apprehensions of my child ever being the slightest burthen to my friends at home, as you will learn by my Will that it is my strict injunctions to my Executuro on no account to send the child home nor even so much as separate it from her mother as I feel assured that the poor child will be much happier brought up as a native than as an European unless she has a father to provide for it. Should I ever be possessed of the means of educating it I know not how I may then be actuated. I am sure you will not blame me if I support and educate my own offspring - it is but natural for me to have the common regards and feelings of other men.

I know not how it was in your time, but the feeling of the present day with regard to illegitimate children are these - Did any Gentleman discover his children by native women, he would immediately be discarded from all society. You will probably ask the question why I took a woman into keeping? I have much to deduce in extenuation of my conduct. When I first went to Benturing, my partner Mr. Winter kept a woman, who had not the greatest command over her passions, and fearful that in some of my weaker moment I might have done what hereafter I should have blamed myself for by injuring Mr. Winter beyond my reparation, as she was the mother of his two children, I was by this induced to keep a girl - further the want of society banished as it were in the jungles of Sumatra, without a soul to converse with or any one to attach my self to, being left at times for nearly a month together by myself - and no one to look after my clothes etc., prepare a comfortable return after a boiling hot days work, and the fear of getting deceased by going with women of the town, who were the greater part of them not very sound; No less than four Gentlemen having at that time left this from severe venerial, was a further inducement for me to keep a woman, do not my dear father take it amiss I have written thus. You must be aware that young men will be young men, so perfect chastity among them almost to an impossibility in this climate. I am proud in saying that my little child promises to be good looking, and as fair as I could justly expect - I feel all the affections for it that a father can feel for a child. I have long thought of broaching this subject to you, fearful that had anything happened me, you would have thought that I had not acted justly towards you.

You seem to "think that my best plan would be to go to Singapore". Ere this you will have learnt my sentiments on the subject of my intentions on the arrival of the Dutch, the only inducement for me to leave this settlement would be the opportunity of weaning myself from the connection I have just mentioned, otherwise Bencoolen has more natural inducements to me than any other place in India - probably on the arrival of the Dutch I be able / with a better grace / to cut the connection, at present it cannot be done, not that I have ever had occasion to find fault with my Girl, on the contrary she has always conducted herself <u>too much</u> to my satisfaction, otherwise I should not feel the compunction that I do feel when I think of the step that I must <u>necessarily</u> pursue sooner or later - getting children without the means of supporting them, is truly a heavy crime; in my humble opinion - under these feelings I am actuated. You may pity me but am sure you will not blame me could you but sympathise with my present feelings. Singapore is at present I am fearful but a poor market for me. James Grant went there a few months back with much better prospects than I could expect, but he returned after going overall or the better of the British Settlements in India and after all returned to poor Bencoolen; the settlement of Singapore is overstocked with traders all cutting each other's throats, for the present I shall remain quiet, until such time as we hear something more final - the Dutch <u>cannot</u> take possession for 6 months to come and probably a twelvemonth - nevertheless we poor monthly writers are to be discharged at the end of this month - I do not know how they will carry on the duties of the place, I can only hope they will give us work and pay us by the section. I must work very hard and save enough cash to discharge all demands before the transfer. I am almost afraid I shall not be able to do it.

I told you poor Tom died out of debt. I did tell you so as I did not wish you to know at the time of his death of his connection with Mrs. N. and a dashing native woman of the town lead into expenses which he otherwise would have avoided. When I left Benturing on my honor I was not indebted one rupee in the settlement more than my monthly bazar bills. I had managed to save as I believe I told you in a former letter 500 R's which went to the liquidation of poor Tom's debts, he was indebted of upwards double that amount besides the exorbitant expences of his funeral - 300 R's more - he had property to double that amount but I did not sell any of it, with the exception of his old coats, the bill of which amounted to about 30 R's. In speaking of his Estate accept my filial thanks for your kindness which it shall ever be my endeavour to deserve, if you peruse the letter I received from the Secretary of Government to me regarding poor Tom's estate, you will find that "the Registrar will call upon me for an inventory of such articles etc., and enter into securities etc.," which was never done by him. Sir Stamford told me that it was merely a matter of form, consequently your enclosure with the letters in my possession will always be sufficient vouchers for any claims hereafter preferred, if there are any.

In all your letters you make mention of 2 pipes of Maderia which you have given directions to be sent, as yet I have seen nothing of them, I wish they had arrived, as I could raise the wind by the sale them. The most advisable thing for me is to remain upon Botany Bay until something turns up, if the Dutch are not too hard upon us, we may still find it worth our while to remain at Bencoolen. The Dutch are not quite so bad as they make them, one bad thing for us, is Bencoolen being put under Padang, they may hereafter make other arrangements, it would certainly be more advantageous for this place being headquarters. I know not what treatment I may expect from them but I believe the native Boms? Bouts? of Padang are treated with the privileges of Europeans. I certainly am not of temperament to put up with maltreatment, having some bile in my system; nothing very extraordinary, after a residence of nearly four years in a climate like Bencoolen, it is too serious a subject to joke upon, at times I shudder at the idea.

I cannot learn from your letter whether you had learnt of my brother's demise previous to the sailing of the Leighton or whether you had written at all by her. I am in expectations that you have done so; the ladies must not take it amiss that I have not written them, it becomes an arduous task to keep up a correspondence with you all at home, but I'll endeavour to do my utmost. I never let an opportunity escape me of letting you hear from me, and particularly at such a crisis. I shall not take any steps without duly weighing them myself and advising with my friends, but at present we are all in a state of great anxiety and suspense. As you have given me Botany Bay for my sole benefit you may depend upon my paying every attention to it, and I hope you will never have cause to complain of your liberallity being abused. I shall forward you the accounts by the Leighton should she be bound for Europe - Tho' I have my doubts, if she will not be taken up by this Government for taking away stores etc. No freight being procurable at this place at present.

You speak of having sent Baskett and me powers of Attorney to act jointly as your agents, I shall ever endeavour to discharge the duty to your satisfaction. I believe Bogle's lease is nearly out for Combong, he has fulfilled his agreement with respect to planting out yearly a certain number of plants. I was speaking to

Baskkett on the subject and he advises your saying that in case of his declining to rent it any longer that you will either let me rent it or give me the superintendance of your share of it, which will I'm assured induce him to continue renting it rather than have another in any way to interfere with him. I know Bogle's feelings so well, he is very tenacious of any interference, particularly so, with his plantations, you cannot under existing circumstances expect so high a rent as 6,000 Sicca R's - but I think we might screw him to 4,500 or 5,000 R's - when be broaches the subject - trust to my acting to the best of my inexperienced abilities. The plantation / Combong / is in very good order, the best plan, without a doubt, is leasing it out for a certain number of years.

I have often regretted not having been quite so punctual in taking copies of my letters to you, for example this is one which I shall not be able to copy, Tho' I particularly wish it, my time not admitting of it, it being nearly midnight. Several others and I may say the greater part of them I have never copied, I should certainly feel a pleasure in having copies of all my letters to you, could you if an opportunity offered let me have <u>all</u> my letters, I will copy them, and if it is your wish they can easily be returned. Your letters to us I have compiled in a Book and it affords me no triffling pleasure when I read some of them of a very late date, they recall circumstances to my mind which I had almost forgotten. I have mentioned to you in the letter that accompanied this, the circumstances of my writing for opium - I can only again regret that it was not sent - I should have made a very good speculation by it - however there is no knowing, perhaps it has been for the best. I have had the Title Deeds of Botany Bay compared with those in the office. A new copy not being necessary, I have not had it done, as it was the Secretary's opinion.

Respecting Robert Perreau I should wish to speak a few words trusting that it may not come to the knowledge of the ladies. Only conceive his having a grown-up daughter / whom he has only within the last four months sent to school/ making her associate with a girl he took but a few weeks back/ what we call goddesses[30]/ She was a reputed one, he generally has one if not two a month, of which he makes a boast, keeping, brutal to relate, his shirt as a trophy of his prowess, these acts are done in the most-faced way, all this time he has nine naked children running about his compound, a spectacle to all passengers, giving continual mirth to the lowest of the Clerks in the office and none of his monthly bills are even discharged tho' drawing nearly 600 R's a month. If a man was ever lost to all shame poor Robert is an instance of it. I have spoken but to no purpose. He drinks like a fish, and as his credit is exhausted with the respectable shopkeepers he has taken to drinking arrack out of the Bazar - truly I believe him Bad!!! [*Pencil cross on page 'R. Perreau' written across, presumably by Chas. Day*].

With regard to emancipating the people I mentioned as being infirm, as yet I have not done it, as it is not their wish, they having no means of supporting themselves, they are however completely left to their own inclinations, having each a small quantity of rice monthly, in every sense of the word they are pensioners - it would be a cruel act after so many years of faithful services to turn them adrift without the means of subsistence - I hope you will give no countenance to a Doctor Bell who may introduce himself by a letter from Baskett; ere this you will have learnt by my letters, what sort of a character this Gentleman is. Should a Mr. Bevines at a future period visit Southampton / and whom you must recollect seeing at Helena of this Civil Service/ any attention that you may have in your power of paying will be but a return for the great attention he has ever shown me at Bencoolen - he is now our second Senior Servant, and a man much respected, tho' at times apt to exceed a glass more than he can bear - he is however a Gentleman!!!!. more than I can say for the aforesaid Dr. Bell who is a Gentlemanly blackguard.

Old Baskett keeps his health as well as ever, if possible he looks younger than when he left this for England, he says that he has written you. Poor Bogle is very much down in the dumps, enough to make him and all others similarly situated, I do not know what I shall do when they discharge me. I cannot get it out of my mind. I believe I have said the same thing over to you at least three or four different points of this scrawl. I am at present sitting writing you this letter by the light or your Pedestal Candlesticks, the hour past one o'clock in the morning. I have been induced to write you thus fully as the Gentleman who was kind enough to take the trouble of bringing your letter out to the plantation informs me that the Padang sails positively tomorrow morning - I am not sure that it will reach the Captain's hands, it must however take its chance. Rose has today been brought to bed of two promissing pupps, poor creature!!

Make my excuses acceptable to the ladies, I will write them by the Leighton, should she be bound for Europe. Let me hear from Charles and Robert, they must now be big boys. I am truly happy in hearing that they promise so well, Vaughan, George & little Johnny must begin to assume a formidable appearance, I mean the two elder ones /however I do not know how it is, but such is the case, I do not feel an equal affection for my brothers as I feel for my sister there is something very endearing in the name. Having so many of the one and only one of the other may in some measure account for it. May God bless them all and their dear parents is my constant prayer. It is truly flattering to me to know that my conduct has been so satisfactory to you. I shall still endeavour to be deserving of it. With filial love and regards to all at Bevis Hill I remain by begging of you to accept the same from your dutiful and very affectionate Son,

Wm. G. Day

½ past one o'clock Sunday morning.

P.S. How does Sir Stamford get on at home, let us hear how he gets on. Mr. Canning[31] by the papers does not seem to be a friend of his. Mr. Prince is now our acting Resident, he is a good man, I should be glad to hear of his getting a pension, his length of service merits it. I have just returned from a visit at Pumattam Ballam, he was condoling with me on the hardships of my case. We are daily in expectations of Captain Mackenzie[32] arrival to be here at the giving over of the settlement.

I have expressed a wish in my former letter for my brother's picture - It is hardly fair of me to make such a request. I leave it completely to your own option - it would certainly afford me many moments of melancholy pleasure to gaze on those features, which I have been accustomed to gaze upon for so many years, from my early childhood to the day of his death, you may almost say we had never been separated, only think what must have been my feelings to have him snatched from me in an hour's warning - it is too much indeed!! Adieu.

Letter 8

In another hand: from Wm. Day 23 March to Bogles renting Combong.

To: Chas. Day, Esquire, Bevis Hill, Southampton, Hants.
From: Wm. G. Day

Botany Bay Plantation
23 rd March 1825

My Dear Father,

I have now per return of Layton the pleasure to acknowledge the receipt of your several letters vitz - Duplicate & Triplicate of the 24th April, 24-12th June, Original & Duplicate 24th June and 15th July, 24 all of which I shall now endeavour to answer.

You appear to wish my trying Singapore as a field for speculation. The only motive I can urge in its favor is the one I have already given in a former letter per ship Padang motives against it I can deduce several - daily examples of adventurers going there, and being obliged to leave it from the place not answering there expectations in fact it is useless for a youngman to go there unless <u>connected or supported</u> by some house or Agency in Calcutta. I think you will find upon enquiry that this is the case, a single trader upon a small capital would I. am fearful do little or nothing - there is an opening in one line which those who have received the education of a Gentleman and have the character of one to support could not avail themselves of - it is that of turning Tavern keeper. I'm sure you would not exactly wish me to fill such a situation and particularly coming from Bencoolen, where I have always been received in the first society. Did I go there otherwise than a merchant I know from those who have been there I should not be received in society, a haughtier class of men are not to be found in India than the Singapore Merchants.

Mr. Prince gave me the option of following the establishment to Singapore but said that he could not secure me my salary after my arrival there - I have consequently not accepted of his offer for these reasons, firstly - I should have been obliged to leave by the first opportunity without being able previously to dispose of my property - and leaving property in the hands of an Agent during these busy times would be sacrificing it all together - Secondly - Did I go there it would be a lottery whether the Resident would have been pleased to employ me; in the case of his not employing me I should have been obliged to return at a very heavy expence to Bencoolen and the communication between this and Singapore is seldom direct, generally via Batavia - which would make it a double expence and thirdly - I am too well aware on what footing I should be received at Singapore did I go there as a monthly writer in Government employ - I should be looked upon the same as the other country born young men sent round at the same time under the same circumstances as myself and as such might naturally expect to be treated after the character I have already given you of the Singapore Merchants. Tho' these young men may not have received the education that I may have had, this nevertheless would not have been taken into consideration - I would rather then remain in Bencoolen a gentleman than be at Singapore considered otherwise then what I am entitled to be.

By remaining at Bencoolen I shall be entitled to a Pension from Government, such being the orders sent from Bengal that "all monthly writers shall have granted to them moderate Pensions", the pension I may expect must be trifling, it is nevertheless a Godsend as I expected that they would have turned us off without giving themselves any further consideration for us. Baskett and Bogle both remain here and it is the advice of all my friends here that I should remain where I am. I hope these reasons will satisfy you that in remaining in Bencoolen is the plan I can best adopt just at present.

You say in your last that "property will rise in value on the arrival of the Dutch" I can only say that Argyle Bonds are for sale at 75 per cent discount and no purchasers - what could I do with the small sum that Botany Bay would at the present moment realise it would not fetch 1500 R's tho' formerly valued at 5,000 R's you would hardly credit such an assertion did it not come from any other source - but I give you my word such is the case and this is the reason. [*This preceding sentence is crossed through in pencil*] Bencoolen is not to be the Presidency - but a Dependency on Padang. The establishment for this place will consequently be trifling. They talk of sending a sergeant and 5 men but that is all nonsence. Nevertheless the Dutch are very loth to take possession as yet they have not done it - not having any troops to spare to send down here to take charge as they are doing but badly at Macassar.

According to the promise contained in my last letter I have enclosed a copy of my will for your perusal and hope that it is such as will be satisfactory to you, it is almost a copy of my former will which I made immediately after the demise of poor Tom - otherwise than nominating you as one of my Executors, I have drawn it as plainly and as short as I could, it cannot be well misunderstood - My other Executor Thomas Williams is old Griffith's son - a man on whose integrity I can safely trust; he is the man I would recommend you appointing in Baskett's place should he like many other poor fellows be carried off too, it is as well to be provided against emergencies. I should not like to act against Robert Bogle unless having someone to advise with and Williams is the man by whose opinion I should probably be guided. Robert Bogle is so deep a hand that I should be obliged to keep the best look out upon him, and he would then probably get to windward of me - Government has reduced my pay by one half from the first of the present month. I come under this lash being one of the Junior Assistants - Why could not Government have reduced a certain percentage on all the monthly writers salaries. Those who are drawing 400 R's a month could better bear these retrenchments than one upon 100 R's - you see how I am situated not being in the Service. Did I venture to murmer against these measures - they would turn me out altogether.

Bogle has according to the spirit of the agreement between you and him regarding the lease of Combong written Baskett to say that at the expiration of the lease he <u>cannot</u> any longer continue to hold it under the present terms, but concluded by saying that upon the present transfer being taken into consideration he will be happy to listen to any proposals that Baskett may make him for renewing the lease - before I make any comments upon the case I must first inform you that there has been a serious quarrel between these two concerning some sales of opium, I know neither the merits nor demerits of the case, - I was consequently requested by Baskett on the receit of Bogles letter to speak to him on the subject and to suggest to B. the propriety of his stating more particularly his reasons for throwing it up, attributing it solely to the expected transfer. I saw B. and told him what I have just stated - he returned for answer that his "letter was completely to the purpose", I then asked him what he would offer to rent yr half share of Combong under existing circumstances to which he answered as follows "I must take time to consider upon it, but you may judge what will be my offer when I tell you that I would not give your father half the amount of the present yearly rent to purchase his half share, out and out, the plantation does not give 300 nuts per day - at this rate it does not pay its expences". This was the whole of the conversation that passed between us at that time - the other morning at a Governor's levee while sitting next to each other, he broached the subject of your "having written him a very serious letter encouraging him to continue renting Combong but you had never so much as hinted at the likelyhood of the settlement being transferred to the Dutch" insinuating as much as that you intended to take him in - I told him that I suppose you had "written him on the state of your property at Bencoolen, and not upon the state of affairs in India" to which he made no further reply. He is an ungrateful fellow!!! is all I can say on the subject.

Baskett has written him requesting of an offer from him otherwise he will himself advance proposals which are /as he intends/ as follows - That I shall go out and live at Combong and take charge of your half share - This alone will be sufficient to make him rent it - as Combong is his principal residence, also for what will he rent the plantation alone? and afterwards ask him for what he will rent your half share of the house? I do not think he has considered the benefit of a comfortable house to live in, he shall not have it under 50 R's a month. If B. only hints to him my taking charge of it that will be a sufficient inducement for B. to come to our terms - he has had the sole undisturbed management of the Plantation for so long a time that he considered it as the whole belonging to him - we must however endeavour to undeceive him - he has reaped the fruits too long.

I have to acknowledge the receipt of the Extract from your accounts - and shall not fail to avail myself of it should it be required tho' it is to be hoped I never shall. I was never called upon by the Registrar to enter into any securities or give in an Inventory. Sir Stamford told me that it was merely a matter of form and as I have never heard anything further from Government, I shall most certainly not broach the subject to them. Your letters which I now have in my possession will always be sufficient for me to substantiate my claim. No pangerams can now make any claim - as that has been done away with from the 1st March 25.

I shall not be able to forward you a copy of the account of Botany Bay as I have been so hard fagged the whole of this month that I have had little or no spare time on hand. I suppose it does not much matter my sending it at all - it will be satisfactory for you to know that it pays its expences hansomely in comparison to its size - the trees are yielding very well and averaging from 300 to 400 a day. I have purchased four head of cattle for manure and intend purchasing more when a good bargain offers as the last.

By this transfer Robert Perreau will be entitled to a very handsome pension. I do not know what his intentions are - the wisest plan for him is to lay bye on his pension in old Bencoolen. If he goes elsewhere be will be lost to all intents and purposes, here his exentricities are known - elsewhere they are not.

I further forward you a letter from yr agents to me on the subject of my application for opium. I'm sorry they did not send it as I should have done very well with it, and by this, time I might have said that I was out of Debt - from Mr. Basketts letter I had every reason to expect that it would have been sent. As yet I have neither seen nor heard of the 2 pipes of wine; you mention in all your letters having given orders for it being sent to me - I really wish that also would have come - at present it would sell for little or nothing.

Baskett has not yet spoken to Prince on the subject of his bond as he is at present too much taken upon with public business, he talks of going from this strait home to Europe. I should consequently suppose that he must have some money otherwise he would not go on his bare pension, this being the case Baskett has determined upon pushing him - I think he has acted very ungenerously. The slaves I have not liberated. They are allowed a small quantity of rice and do what work they can, such as weeding the roots of the young trees etc. Could you send me out poor Tom's inscription stone - at home it costs a trifle where as in Calcutta it will stand me in upwards of 300 R's by the time it reaches Bencoolen, I shall be most happy to pay it out of my own pocket, this is not a hint for you to send it out - I shall really feel gratefully obliged by your complying with it. It is nothing more than poor Tom deserves from my hand / fail not to send it.

Should John Edwards be still at home on the receit of this, thank him on my account for his kind letter. I do not write according to his request, but anxiously wait for his next epistle which I shall not fail to answer. I'm truly sorry to hear that Mrs. Day has been so very unwell. Remember me to Fred Minchin and his brother if they are still at Clayfield and all friends and old domestics. I have written the ladies a letter between them, in the busy times they will excuse my not writing so fully as I otherwise should do, they attribute it to the right reason for I begin to detest the sight of pen and paper. You write me that your last letter was written on your birthday, may you long live to enjoy many happy returns of that day is ever my sincerest prayer. Poor old Rosa I am very fearful will not live much longer, I begin to perceive a daily change in the poor creature. Could the poor creature but speak I'm sure she would sincerely join me in kind love and effectionate regards to you all at Bevis Hill.1

Believe me to be
My dear Father
Your very dutiful & affectionate son,
Wm. G. Day.

Included with William's letter of 23 March 1825

Copy of a letter from Messrs Ferguson & Co. 18 November 1824.

To: Wm. G. Day, Bencoolen

Calcutta
18th November, 1824

Sir,

We have only two days since received your letter of the 14th March last. We regret that it will not be convenient for us to send you the opium you wish for our latest from your father is dated 31st May at which time from the intended transfer of your settlement to the Dutch he appears to have altered his ideas on the propriety of laying out Capital at Bencoolen.

We are etc.,

Sgd. Ferguson

A true copy Wm. G. Day.

A true copy of the last Will and Testament of William Grant Day of Bencoolen

LET ALL MEN KNOW that by these presents, I William Grant Day of Bencoolen Do hereby in this my last Will and Testament being now of sound state of mind / bequeath to my only sister Emma Amelia Day the daughter of Charles and Fanny Day of Southampton, and my natural Daughter Ellen Day of Bencoolen, the whole of my property to be divided between them as here below stated vitz:

Two thirds to the aforesaid Emma Amelia Day her heirs and One third to my aforesaid daughter Ellen Day & her heirs -

I have made this provision for my daughter with the intention of her being brought up as a native and on no account to be sent home to my friends in Europe; these are my strict instructions, as I consider it will be better for her future welfare and happiness thro' life -

I do hereby further bequeath to my mother Incie Jannin and to my Housekeeper See Jeune / to each of them a legacy of 500 Rupees. To my housekeeper See Jeune I hereby transfer my two slaves See Gylar and See Gambos.

It is my particular request that none of my trinkets be disposed of but sent home to my friends in Europe, with a lock of my hair, and further that my body be lay'd next to my late brother Tom.

My father Charles Day of Southampton and Thomas Williams of Bencoolen I do hereby appoint as joint Executors and I leave it to the discretion of my Executor here to take such steps for the disposal of my property as he may think proper.

Signed this 8th day
of March at Signed Wm. G. Day
Botany Bay Plantation

In the presence of
Witness: Sd. Jas. Grant
John Christie

Fort Marlbro'
8th March 1825

A true copy
Wm. G. Day.

Letter 9

On cover: Mr. Wm. Day 10th Nov. 1825

10th Novr. 1825

My dear Father,

We have all met with a sad disappointment in not being able to send our letters by the Borneo. She left this two months ago for the Northern ports under the promise of touching on her return at Rat Island for letters. I'm fearful she must have gone past. I had several letters in readiness for her, but as many material things have transpired since their date I have sat down to give you the particulars of my former letters, as also the particulars which have but within these few days transpired.

I must first inform you of our plans with Bogle regarding Combong. He refused to rent it at above 1,200 RS/ Guilders payable in Bencoolen per year. Mr. Baskett has consequently induced me to try your half share on the same terms as Ble. has held of you for the Last two years. 3,600 R's being at present idle I have taken it upon those terms but trust should the produce not be sufficient to cover the rent and expences you would not exact the difference - but should any triffling profit accrue therefrom I trust it will be considered as mine. I do not wish to hold exactly upon a lease but to be considered as superintending it. I pledge myself faithfully to remit the whole of the produce either to Europe or Calcutta, as opportunities and the state of the markets may admit, but disposing of some of the produce at Bencoolen for the purpose of defraying the monthly expences, for at present I'm enjoying no monthly income, my pension not being confirmed by the supreme Government.

I have submitted for your satisfaction "A list of slaves belonging to Combong", "Monthly Abstract of rice and pay at Combong" and "an Estimate of Botany Bay".

I assumed charge of Combong from the 1st instant / today I have accomplished my One & Twentieth year / I have received conjointly with Mr. Baskett on yr account the produce of spice from Combong from July to the 1st instant, had the Borneo touched here we should have sent it home, but must now wait for another opportunity, but when that will be I cannot form the most distant calculation. I rent / or if you please to term it superintend / Combong under many disadvantages. The present <u>very high price</u> of rice 10 R's a bag with the prospect of its very soon becoming higher; I must endeavour to get a consignment from Bengal as carrying on a plantation at the that expence must naturally make me a considerable sufferer. In increasing the p1antation yearly / as either renter or superintendent receive no benefit, it was far different with Bogle, as any increase he made was for your mutual good, I shall however continue to increase the plantation, should the 20 hands be adequate to keep the old plantation in order and carry on the new one, tho' I'm fearful the late increase made by Bogle will be as much as the 20 hands will be able to keep in cu1tivation.

There is also another disadvantage by which you will also become a sufferer - having so small a flock of cattle, as that kind or stock is at present at a very low rate / owing to all out convicts being about to leave / we have proposed purchasing about 15 to 20 head more; they are now selling at 10 P[33]. a head whereas formerly 18 & 20 P. was considered a moderate price - by the papers enclosed you will perceive that Combong has upwards of 2,000 trees including the old and new plantation, it will consequently be morally impossible to keep a plantation of this extent in any state of cultivation with a flock of ten head of cattle. I hope you will see the propriety of this measure for cattle ought always to realise to the proprietor on the resale or them a profit and not a loss as you may be induced to suppose from the account of your Combong flock given by Ble. but you must not give credit to all that Ble. may do, Ble. has a flock at Combong of probably 60 or 80 head but he says they are from his pen at Cobone Baruse - at Co. Baruse he cannot have less than 200 head, from this you may judge if he ever purchased the whole of this stock at 18 or 20 P. a head, if the truth was known they belong to the concern of Chas. Day & Co.

I should prefer by far your allowing me to superintend than renting Combong as the future sales of spices are precarious. I do not wish to charge anything for the Superintendence, but leave it to yourself to remunerate me hereafter as you may think proper, being idle I have been induced to look after your property tho' I must in some measure sacrifice Botany Bay by being obliged to live in the country, but not at Combong house. After much trouble Ble. has made me an allowance for my share of the dwellinghouse, he allows me 25 R' s a month and instead of taking up my quarters with him I have the house at Titsnest free of rent which belongs to Wm. Lewis. I hold it on condition of keeping it in repair. Ble's allowance is but a shabby one as I'm obliged to build my out offices at Titsnest as they have been allowed to go to ruin, the house rent from Ble. will barely defray my expences at the other place, however there is one accommodation to myself, as I shall be better able occasionally to run into Botany Bay than if I was at Combong having but a small stud.

Mr. Baskett remitted you a bill of 45£ the other day on acct. of spices sold to Captain Ross of tho Borneo which I suppose will be most acceptable, you must however not expect or consider that sum as any criterion by which you may judge of your monthly produce, as it was during the close harvest and it was not the nutmegs but cloves which realised the amount / the Bill was exactly the amount proceeds of one months produce/

Bgl. informs me that Combong has just been thoroughly manured. I must ascertain this point from the people as should he not have done it I shall consider it a breach of his agreement with you "to give up the plantation in good order" which cannot be the case without it. He must in this latter case manure it with his own hands and his own expence. Ble. complained to Mr. Baskett that you had been much dissatisfied with him respecting not "remitting you money" he has sent you 4,000 R's in a Bill per Borneo, so he tells me!!!!

The next subject to which I wish to call your attention is respecting your promised credit for 5 chests of opium. I much regret that it was not sent down this season for a handsome thing might have been made of it. The principal inducement for my stopping here, banished as it were from all friends and acquaintances is in the hopes of making something in that trade, at least gaining a livelyhood. If any unforseen accident was to happen to you / which God forbid / to prevent my obtaining a credit I should immediately leave Bencoolen for one of the British Eastern Establishments, the Dutch Service holds out no hopes. I rendered my services and they offered me 50 R's a month, much less than what a common soldier in the English Service gets a month, besides his rations and liquor. The supreme Government has most shamefully stopped the pensions of all those who have not served a period of fifteen years, it has astonished everyone. They have reverted to an old order of many years back and seem not to have taken the transfer into their consideration. I can only attribute it to the illiberallity of the present Lord[34], had the Marquis[36] been here it would have been otherwise. We have not however, let them shake us off so easily for a memorial has been addressed by us to the Supreme Government and I do not think that they will be able to refuse it to us - We are only 5 in number, the amount would not be 300 R's monthly.

Since I have been from home I never knew what it was to be in want until the retrenchment of my pension, for I have always had until the present time something monthly besides my plantation, it is useless to murmur, it is to be hoped that it is all for the best, it now only remains for the Dutch to levy such a duty as will make it no longer worth my time to care for my plantation, and then there will be an end of cares and troubles in Bencoolen, the transfer of this settlement will always give me a claim upon the British Government and to them I shall trust when I can no longer hold onto my mother. One and all of us have a dismal prospect before us. Both Bogle and Baskett think of moving. There are only 7 of us who have been obliged to stay behind, the Dutch completely keep to themselves, they have not done us yet the complement of asking us to dinner.

The next subject I wish to revert to is regarding the allowance of 50 R's and not 50 Drs. which you mentioned in your letters per Repulse, I continued to draw after your order to stop same. I am aware of my error and from the moment I received your last letters upon that subject I discontinued it.

Your old friend Mr. Prince did nothing for me. I believe he was too much taken up with his own consequence to pay me any kind of attention or make you any return for his obligations to you. He took particular care to strike me off the books one of the first, and put me upon a subsistence allowance of half of my pay and made me work notwithstanding.

In all your letters you mention two pipes of Madeira. As yet I have seen nothing of them, they would be most acceptable I assure you in these hard times.

The jacket and shoes fit me remarkably well, they came most a' propos tho' quite unexspected at the time. I want words to express my thanks to you for the broche made of Mrs. Day's hair and be assured that I shall ever keep it for both your sake and the ring will be equally dear to me.

Express to Mrs. Day my sincere sense of gratitude for her tender concern for my poor brother Tom, it is truly gratifying to me to know that I possess her esteem and tell her as the strongest proof I can give her of the high value I set on it, will be to endeavour ever to continue to deserving of it, the broche and ring are both double dear to me for both her sake and poor Tom's. Should I have time I must thank her in a separate letter, if not do you for me. I intend to drink Miss Perreau's health & many happy returns of this day to her, I shall never forget this time 5 years back when she accomplished her 50 years sitting round the family fire at Bevis Hill and surmizing where I should be this time 5 years, it is the most dismal birthday that I have yet witnessed, I'm happy in a good state of health thank God, and hope you all at home enjoy the same.

Robert has left this per Rupulse for Singapore, as yet we have had no letters but heard of his arrival at Penang. In going over has got rid of many incumbrances, but all that I could do, I could not persuade him from taking two hulking sons of his round with him, the remainder of his family are here quite unprovided for. He ought to have remained here and availed himself of his pension one half of his allowances, for Robert is too old to be gagging in an office, his eyes are very weak.

The estimate of Botany Bay of which I enclose a copy, is the estimate I gave to Mr. Prince. I do not know if we have any chance of a remuneration, I could not get hold of Bogle's estimate of Combong, but I know that the net Income given in as one estimate was, 4,444 Dollars spanish.

Poor old Baskett has met with a sad loss in the death of Mrs. Banks alias Mother Baskett. She was attacked with a fit of cholera and expired in a few hours, for these two months that dredful complaint has been raging at Bencoolen, 10 to 12 a day have died out of one bazarre, and the small pox is also raging but not many have fallen victim to it being very mild.

Should you have an opportunity of sending any thing to Bencoolen you may send me some common salts as this sickly season has completely run me out of that valuable medicine, and nowadays we have no medical store to resort to supply our wants. The Doctor charges 5 R's a visit and for medicines at the same ratio. Alas poor Bencoolen!!!!

Make my old present to the little ones and kiss all round. So often I think of them and of all at Bevis hill. I send you a sketch of my cottage at Botany Bay taken by Doctor Scott of the Repulse an old shipmate of mine, he has promised to draw it on a larger scale and make a higher finished drawing of it by the time he gets to England. I have given him your address, he may or he may not send it, however, there is no harm in enclosing this rough sketch as I am persuaded you will feel some satisfaction in knowing that it came from your affectionate son,

Wm. G. Day.

Letter 10

Stamped Ship Letter Dover. Also Post Mark Bishop Mark 10 F Noon and another stamp partly illegible Aug. 12 1826.

To Chas. Day Esquire, Bevis Hill, near Southampton, Hants, England.
To the Care of Messrs Ladbroke & Co., via Batavia, Cornhill, London.

Bencoolen
16 Jany. 1826

My Dear Father,

I have just stolen a moment to write to you a few lines, to acquaint you of the turn of affairs at Old Bencoolen. In my last letter dated a short time back I was busyly engaged at Combong and rusticating in the country. From the first of the present month I have pursued another line again. I am a "quill driver" in the Govt. Service upon 100 R's a month, this however does not prevent me from attending to your interests in the country as I take a run out there every other evening and return to the office the following morning. I have no sinecure in the Dutch employ, they pay you for your time and they will have it; hours of attendance from 9 to 4 whereas during the English reign it was 10 to 3 o'clock. Having no other monthly income than the produce of Botany Bay and Rice at 6 Drs. a month obliged me tho' very very much against my inclinations to enter the most despicable service in India. I have only entered it in a temporary way until something better turns up. Appo bouli boit!!!!

On the 4th inst. the settlement was thrown into a ferment by a coffree[38] running a muck. Poor little Tom William (old Mr. Griffiths' son) as Magistrate went to apprehend him - the peons[37] on reaching the place where the man was committing devastation all fled and left poor W. who was on horse back, unarmed, to the mercy of the coffree who immediately speared him through the body - he would have escaped had not his horse fallen in turning him round - he expired 2 hours after - most sincerely regretted by every one. He was my most particular friend. On his death bed he appointed me Guardian to his son and an executor in consort with Robt. Bogle and Mr.Wain to his will, he particularly requested that I should be allowed to take charge of his plantation, and as he was at the time of his death acting as Agent for the greater part of those who have left, you can well conceive to yourself that to do justice to the trust confided in me I must not be idle, he comes in the list of the first rate planters as his property is very extensive and at the same time in full bearing. Make my kindest regard to Mr. and Mrs. Griffiths when you write to them - and tell him that poor Tom died in the peace and good wll of us all. Bogle has succeeded Williams as Magistrate with the rank and title of Assistant Resident!!! He has left the country altogether and is obliged to live in town, and has sent out an European to Superintend his property.

With regard to Combong you will not under my present circumstances oblige me to rent it. I promise to give my attention as hitherto, to receive the produce, remit the same to you by every convenient opportunity, and I trust to your liberallity for any compensation you may think me deserving of, for my trouble. Bogle says that he has sent you cash by this opportunity, and Basket has also remitted the three months produce he received previous to my assuming charge. Combong is very low 500 nuts a day at the utmost we are however all much in the same way.

I have been obliged to subscribe on our joint account One pecul of Nutmegs, half from Combong and half from Botany Bay - for the purpose of forming a fund in England to enable them to fight for the "remuneration and indemnfication" it comes very hard upon me as a young planter, there was no distinction made, one and all subscribed the same, tho' I fought hard against it. I wished to have subscribed according to my means, but the majority went against me and I was obliged to give way.

You will hear strange accounts from Bencoolen but no less strange than true, they are levying duties, taxes on all kind of property, stamps brought into use etc. etc. etc., fact they are oppressing us, in every possible way. Of Old Bencoolenites, there only remain five of us, we keep to ourselves, as the Dutchmen are so great a set of blackguards that they are not fit company for a gentlemen. The public journals will teem with the acts of injustice and oppression daily taking place under this Govt., they have no cordial friend in H.R. Lewis (who begs to be kindly remembered to you and the ladies), he leaves this in a day or two for Batavia. Old Mr. Baskett has completely recovered and is now well and hearty.

Since Robert Perreau left this - not a soul has received a line from him tho' by letters which I have received from Singapore I learn that he is still out of employment but enjoying his full salary. I have written once or twice to him, I suppose he has forgot me.

Try your interest through your friend Mr. Ladbrooke to get me an appointment to this place from Holland, it would not be attended with very great trouble and an appointment from home is much thought of in the Dutch Service. H.R. Lewis hinted this to me. Will you think of it. If H.R.L. is not reinstated in the English Service it is his intention to come out with an appointment from Holland. I am studying Dutch. I hope to be able to understand something of it shortly. Think seriously of my proposition. I must think of doing something better than fagging upon 100 R's a month, which I have been doing for these 5 years and a half.

Make my most dutiful and affectionate regards to Mrs. Day and Miss Perreau and love to my brothers and my sister Emma. In my present low state of spirits I often shed a tear when I think of the happy happy days spent round the fire side at Bevis Hill and think of my banishment in a foreign country all my best friends leaving others dying around me, it is a truly distressing thing. Of all my many old friends there now only remain, Young James Grant, we are and have always been like brothers. If he has the ill luck to be carried off then I shall be miserable indeed! You may think I romance but when you again see H.R. Lewis only ask him how he left us.

I have not received a letter from you since those I sent by the Repulse, I conclude they must be at Singapore.

I am very anxious for an answer respecting my request to you for the credit of Opium. I must, I am sorry to say, remain in Bencoolen, time flies fast and I must begin to look about me very sharp, I shall be an old man before I know where I am.

Believe me to be my dear Father,
Your very affectionate son,
Wm. G. Day.

Letter 11

Endorsed in another hand: from Wm. Day 14 April 1826

To: Chas. Day Esquire, Bevis Hill, Southampton, Hants
To the Care of Messrs Ladbroke & Co., Bankers, Cornhill
Per Benong via Batavia Wm. G Day.

Bencoolen
14th April 1826

My Dear Father,

Your letter dated 6th May 1825 and addressed to Mr. Baskett and myself reached me two days ago, as also another under date 31st May 1825. These are the only ones I have received near a twelvemonth. I mean to say, since the arrival of the Repulse in June last, your silence gave me great anxiety I was almost fearful that some meloncholy news was near at hand.

Your letter dated 8th May in which you expressed a desire that in case of Bogle's refusing to rent your share of Combong that I should assume the charge and management of the same, you must ere this have learnt that we had anticipated your wishes. I entered in charge / as I mentioned in a former letter / of Combong from the month of November last, and that Bogle had agreed to make me an allowance for my share of the dwellinghouse, but since that period matters have taken another turn. A vacancy occuring in the Secretary's office I applied for the same and my application was accepted upon a salary of R's 100 this step was not taken previous to my taking the opinion of my good friend Baskett - at that time I had not a rupee coming in, but merely the produce of Botany Bay, my pension being stopped. I thought it most advisable to accept of a salary from Government, it was with a very heavy heart that I did it for I was aware of the nature and difference of the service to which I had been accustomed necessity has no law. I am consequently obliged to run out twice a week and look after the people in the country, my time and other business not admitting of my visiting it oftener, as I should wish to do.

Having since January falling into no trifling share of the business of the place by the death of my particular friend Tom Williams / this is the gentleman I recommended to you in case of any accident happening to Baskett / poor fellow he was speared through the body by an intoxicated coffrey while in the execution of his duty as Magistrate. I have lost in him my very best friend in Bencoolen. On his death bed he requested of me in particular from his other executors to take charge of his plantations and his family until such time as his son returns to this country, such a request from him I could not refuse to comply with - by which I have fallen into such a multiplicity of business that I assure you ever since his death I have not had one single day to myself, this is only one part of the accumulation of my business, the whole of these Gentleman who have left their property here have made me their agent and left me in charge of the greater part of the houses in Bencoolen.

I have had also an accumulation of public business, by the death of the head assistant of my office, I have now to carry on the whole business of the office, my premier being a most egregious fool / begging his pardon / and knows little or nothing of the business of an office - merely knows how to sign his name. I am the only assistant in the office - with the exception of Raddin Canims son, who has been to Calcutta for his education and knows just enough of English to make himself understood. I have to dispose and keep the accounts of Govrs. stamps and postage - but my most laborious task is holding the "Vendre" or public auction, this was held by poor William, and he has left bills due to the amount of R's 16,000, the whole of which I have to collect. I am only Klerck to the Vendre, the Secretary is the "Vendra Meesta". I have no responsibility, but all the trouble we have had lately made some large sales, as there has been a second emigration to Singapore in the Mary, a ship taken up by Wm. Lewis for the purpose of taking the coffrees and convicts, but the Netherlands Govt. have interfered and the vessel thrown upon L's hands, a great fuss has been made and it is supposed that our Govt. / The English / will be obliged to take notice of it.

The Netherlands Govt. have levied duties and taxes and of every description. Upon spices they have levied the "triffling" as they call it, duty of R's 9 per pecul upon their own flag but double upon a foreign one. On Magey Rice 1 Rupee per bag - on Opium Rs 300 per chest and so on, where ever they go devastation and ruin invariably follow them. Our present resident is much disliked, a most arbitrary fellow, does just as he pleases, and makes a mocery of justice. The charge of boat hire has risen to double the amount of what was charged by the former Govt. They have levied a transfer tax of 6 per cent upon the sale of all property besides increasing the Vendu charges which generally amount from 18 to 20 percent upon the whole, when a man wishes to dispose of a house and is obliged to put it up to Auction, he losses nearly 25 per cent upon the value of his property. A private individual not being able to hold an Auction, many individuals who have left this, have been obliged to dispose of their property as I have just stated, in the hope of being indemnified from home. I much fear they will be sadly disappointed. Houses that were sold for 20,000 R's will not now fetch 4,000 R's, property of every description has equally decreased in value. Of the old standard inhabitants of Bencoolen, these only remain, Baskett, Bogle, James Grant and myself not a soul more, I do assure you.

The produce of Combong is at present very low and has been so since I had charge of it. Your share is seldom or ever exceeded 400 nuts a day, this last week it has not been 300 per day. I am afraid Bogle uses some unfair measures with me. Such as bribing the Gourdon, he being the person who divides the daily produce, the produce of every week is regularly sent to Botany Bay. With regard to Bogle's remittances, he told me himself that he had got Bills on Europe in your favor for the greater part of the amount of his debt due to you for the rent of Combong at 1s. 11d. for the Sicca Rupee, so he wanted to persuade me, to my knowledge it was 1s. 11d. for the Guilder, what has he told you? Since last November the whole of Combong plantation has been manured and the show of fruit is very promising. The Cloves are again in fruit and in three months we shall have an harvest of them. Baskett has told me that he has written you very fully by this opportunity and has recommended me to your consideration for the trouble I have been obliged to take on account of Combong, this matter I leave completely to you and Mr. Baskett. I can only say that in these hard times any triffle is acceptable.

I am sorry to say that Tom's debt to Mr. B. still remains unpaid. I am not exactly right in mentioning Tom's name only as we jointly contracted the amount. I feel particularly thankful to Mr. B for not having ever pushed me for a settlement, he told me that he intended writing you on the subject, and explain matters, this is not hint to ask you to pay if off for I hope by the time an answer to this will have reached you I shall have been enable to pay it off. I am well aware that you have sufficient demands on your purse, and any such encroachment you can ill afford. I trust however that you will not think from this debt not being settled that I have been throwing away my money upon, as you say "wine at 30 Rupees a dozen" or any other extravagance. I think, without any flattery to myself, that none of my friends, for example Robt. Bogle, can alledge such a thing against me, during the English time many young men of my own class, with much higher salaries, and who had been much longer in the country, did not carry the appearance nor keep the company which I did, the greater part of the civilians who are now to the eastward, there is scarcely one of them with whom I have not contracted the closest intimacy. I am speaking of the Bachelors / and who would not if I choos' d to leave poor Bencoolen be most happy to offer me a situation under them, but I am afraid that at Bencoolen I must remain. I feel somehow as if linked with her destiny, if she falls why I must fall too, when I reflect on the many happy days which I have passed with my Bencoolen friends, as also those to which I have also passed in the society of your domestic little circle at Bevis Hill, when I reflect on these, I cannot avoid feeling some pain, I can scarce refrain a tear, in thinking that those happy days are never to return.

The only companion that I now have, is young James Grant, we have ever been the best of friends, and I hope shall continue so, we equally feel the unfortunate change of the whole settlement of Englishmen who were here this time 12 month, the whole of them have left some with fear, others from necessity, and some from disgust at the new administration and there remains but a solitary few of us as we call ourselves <u>four</u> in number. Bogle not being included, as he is too well known that he is the newscarrier at headquarters and the origin of a great deal of mischief amongst <u>us</u>, for this he is discarded.

Your old friend Mr. Prince cut a caper at Padang, and has managed to find a husband for the amiable Mrs. Sealy / his daughter of noted fame / She is about to be led to the hymeneal alter by the chief justice of Sumatra, Mr. Dahans. Prince gave it out to his friends here that he had long ago settled his accounts with you, and that he thought you had behaved hardly towards him. So much for the old west coast friendships.

With respect to the Opium from Calcutta, I have merely to say that I leave it to yourself, and had it arrived when I expected I might by this time have been out of debt, the only traders who now remain are Baskett and Bogle and if Bogle is confirmed in the service, he cannot either directly or indirectly trade, it would be at the risk of his appointment. I am not anxious to have any this year, but certainly should things carry a good appearance this season, I should like to try my fortune the ensuing one. By that time I shall have been in the Country seven years, and as yet I have / now passed five / and not done one single thing. To be candid I was most sadly disappointed.

The two pipes of Maderia have not to this day come to hand. God knows where it could have travelled to, half over India and back again.

Do not be under any tribulation about my sending the dog Rosa back to England. I recollect saying something about it, but you could not have thought me in earnest. I was merely joking.

Robert Perreau has completely lost himself at Singapore, worse than he was in Bencoolen, he is living in the Bazare. I hear this from other friends as I have not received a line from him, although I have written him four or five times. He is a sad fellow.

I am very sorry to hear of Mrs. Day's and Miss Perreau' s bad state of health: do not fail to make my most affectionate regards to them both, and do assure them that notwithstanding my not having written them, that still I do not forget them, nor can I ever do so after the many parental kindness I have ever experienced at their hands, I wish I could but prove my professions of esteem for them otherwise than by bare words, but I trust they know my heart, and will take the word for the deed. I still live in the hopes of seeing better days. I was talking just now of Robert Perreau. You say that Miss P. has succeeded to her uncle's property, it would be a thousand pities did she throw it away on her worthless nephew, endeavour to instill into her mind that Robert by his length of service is now entitled to a pension of £350 per annum. whenever he chooses to apply for it, and do not let her be led away with any idea that Robert's debts are so very enormous. Those who were fools enough to allow him to contract these debts, let them suffer and not his family, anything she might give or leave to him would be completely thrown away, only conceive a man of his rank still drawing 500 R's a month, living in a Singapore Bazar like a native. I feel quite ashamed of him, and what must Miss P. feel did she hear of such a thing. Robert, can never want wherewith to subsist upon, when you consider that he is entitled to half his pay as a pension for life.

I must draw to a conclusion as my paper warns me. With sincere regards of affection to all the family circle at Bevis Hill and with prayers for their welfare and happiness I remain My dear Father,

Your very affectionate Son,

Wm. G. Day.

Letter 12

Endorsed in another hand Wm. Day 10 September 1826

To: Charles Day, Esquire, Bevis Hill, Southampton, Hants
Bencoolen, 10 Septr. 1826 Wm. G. Day

Bencoolen
10 Septr. 1826

My Dear Father,

Since my last great changes have tooken place. I sincerely wish it was in my power to say they were for the better. Our establishment is daily being reduced. I need only mention that the strength of our garrison does not amount to 50 men, where necessity has obliged Government to reduce their Military establishment, during the present very disaffected state of the settlement; it may fairly be concluded that these arrangements are precussory to the abandonment of the place altogether. This is the general opinion. Under these circumstances I cannot hope to enjoy the small salary allowed me for any great length of time, my dismissal is not far distant, I have however this assurance, that my services can ill be dispensed with, as long as public duty is carried on. It would be difficult for me to tell you what I am, so numerous are my callings. The dutch certainly do not pay their servants for nothing.

Among the many acts of opression daily exercised, it will suffice if I only mention one, and I leave you to judge whether we poor Bencoolen planters have or have not reason to complain. Every measure as yet adopted tends to the rapid ruin of the country. So short sighted is their policy, but let me resume the subject of "opression". A system of torture has been introduced for the purpose of extorting evidence in cases of murder.

You will I suppose hardly credit that a civilysed Govt. could resort to such measures. The fact however is too true. Mr. Robert Bogle who enforces and superintends these tortures has had the audacity to deny it, I have myself been an eye witness. The "Inquisition room" adjoins my office, and the shrieks of the poor unfortunate creatures are heard far around. What must my feelings be sitting in the adjoining room. Is it to be wondered at that all classes of people are emigrating.

Mr. Prince is at present at Bencoolen, sent down by the Bengal Govt. to inquire into the reasons for not allowing the Natives to leave the place, he is empowered with full authority to take away all those who may wish to leave. The Dutch Govt. had on a former occasion resisted it, for this purpose has Mr. P. again visited Bencoolen. Baskett and myself received a letter from Mr. Prince enclosing copy of a letter from you to Ferguson & Co., wherein you authorised us "to deliver up to the order of Fairlie Bonham & Co., Mr. John Prince's bond to me for Dollars 48,000 which we have accordingly done".

The plantation at Combong since I have had charge has seldom exceeded 300 nuts a day as your share, I am fearful as I have all along said to you that Mr. Bogle pampers with the people. As to the cloves I have not received ten bamboos[38]. Certainly the season has been particularly unfavourable owing to the dry weather coming on so early, as soon as the wet season setts in we may naturally expect an increase in the produce. By the first favorable conveyance you may expect to have a remittance of spices. We are expecting the Borneo.

We have received letters from England stating Sir Stamford Raffles having been appointed a Commissioner to enquire into the claims of the Bencoolen planters and advising us all to sell and trust in the indemnification. This plan is yet in contemplation of being followed up so far having not yet heard anything official on the subject. Some have already begun, I am thinking of doing the same, but not just yet. I have been obliged to sell my spices at ps60 per pecul and that I considered a great bargain, in fact there is a complete stagnation to all business. My plans at present are to continue here as long as it is possible, but I do not think that it can exceed one year or eighteen months, unless some very great political change takes place. Even old Baskett is talking of making a move. My partner at Benturing, Mr. Winter sales off in two or three days, with a view of leaving the settlement. In this case James Grant and myself will be the only two Englishmen left behind. Bogle's conduct has been so shameful that no one acknowledges him as an Englishman. I cannot speak of him in terms desirable enough. So past all conception has been his behavior. He is deeply involved in Calcutta Union to the tune of 50,000 Rupees. He sent for opium and 1000 bags of rice from Clatie's house as also requesting them to send down his daughter which the house has taken no notice of.

Since commencing this letter I have learnt that Mr Prince and the Resident have come to a paper war respecting the Coffrees. The whole of the business will now come before Parliament when Bogle's name will be often mentioned not much to his credit.

I have been obliged to build a smoking house for grains and my own spices. Baskett consented to the plan, and has sanctioned my charging you with half the expences. When next you will receive your account, if you object to it, you can run your pen through it, however the place was built as much for your good as mine.

The Dutch are doing everything to drive the people away, taxes and duties are exacted on everything. What do you think of a rupee a bag on Rice and 300R's upon a chest of opium, the charges of boat hire and wharfage raised 50 per C. higher than ever during the English time. They are so miserably poor that they are under the necessity of enforcing these regulations to enable them to carrying on the monthly expences, at Java the Government is equally as short of cash, the Dutch have lately met with a serious defeat in battle with the insurgents, they have collected all the troops they possibly can with the intention of making an effort to crush them if they are unsuccessful. There is no doubt that they will be obliged to recall all their forces from Sumatra and concentrate all their strength at headquarters. In this case poor Bencoolen will be abandoned for a time but whenever they find it convenient to re-establish themselves they will do it, there is the misfortune, if they would leave us altogether we should be most happy at the riddance, under any other circumstances it would not be desirable.

As to my former idea of doing something here in the Opium way, I have almost abandoned, as a man requires large funds on the spot to defray duties etc., before he can dispose of an item of it. Should any thing happen to old Baskett, which God Forbid, there might be an opening for me, as the natives must have opium let the price be what it may. It is only on his opium that the old Gentleman can make anything by, and that is but triffling - 10 chests a year is much as is consumed under present circumstances.

One of our greatest causes of complaint is the "transfer duty" a duty which exacts from the seller of 6 per C. upon all fixed property, another most grevious subject of complaint is the interference of the orphan chamber in all Estates intestate or not, they will have something to say, and give the executors so much annoyance as to oblige them to throw it up, and then they take the whole of it to themselves and nothing more is heard of the estate.

The time that has elapsed since I had the pleasure of hearing from you appears to me an age - did you but know the pleasure it always affords me at the receit of a letter from you, in these unfavourable times, I do not think you would fail to let me hear from you once a year, it is now upwards of a year and I have not received a line. I am daily in the hopes of hearing from you, but ship after ship has arrived and no letter from you. I have been punctual in writing by every opportunity, you cannot tax me with forgetfulness for I assure you Bevis Hill is the constant companion of my thoughts. In moments of philosophic meloncholy (if I may be allowed to use the expression) how often do I not wish from the bottom of my heart that I could but revisit the comfortable home, where I have passed the happiest of happy days amongst you - how great the change between those times and the present - I find many very unpleasant and disagreeable circumstances attending all business, but I am almost tired with the language of complaint against the evils of this world for the most favorable situations are not free from them. Appo bouli boit! as we say in Malays. With kindest love and regards to all at home, Believe me, My dear Father, Yrs very affectionately,

Wm. G. Day.

P.S. Before I conclude do not let me forget to send my kind remembrances to all old friends - such as Captn. and Mrs. Bullen, Fiotts, John Edwards, etc. I have only had one letter from John since my stay in India "out of sight out of mind". I must not also forget Charles Simpson, remember me most affectionately to him as also to his wife and little ones - Kacaffoga. I suppose he must now have ½ a dozen of Kacaffoga's. The Boyer's also are my old friends. I received a letter from Robert Perreau, from Singapore, apprixing me of his good fortune of being considered an Extra Concircuted Servant. I am glad to hear it, this gives him a provision for his life, as whenever he is tired of the service he has his pension to look to. I memorialized regarding my pension, but with no success. I have given that up as lost - again Adieu -

Letter 13

Endorsed: from Wm. Day 23 Oct. 1826

Bencoolen
23rd Octobr. 1826

Dear Father

I wrote to you a short time back on account of the sad state of affairs of poor Bencoolen, and what I expected would shortly take place; my expectations have been more than fully realised - for I had only anticipated a reduction of my salary whereas by late orders from Batavia this Residency is reduced to a Post holdenship - and I am in common with one and all "Honorably discharged from his Netherlands Majesty's Service, my services being no longer required". It burst upon us like a thunderbolt, not one days notice was given, for on the 30th Septr. the orders were issued and I was without any further warning thrown out of my situation. What I am now to do God alone knows. I have met with (lately) many reverses but none have so materially affected me as this last blow, the prospect of Govt. employ is now no longer to be hoped for, and as to private employ that is as hopeless. Trade is worse than all - as to looking for support from my plantation, under present circumstances, it does but hardly pay itself - produce has fallen in the market 500 pr. C. owing to the high Export duty of 25 pr C. per pecul. I fain would sell off, but fixed properties have fallen 95 4/5 per C. since the transfer, moveable properties 85 Pr C. I am anxious to move, but these unsurmountable obstacles - and when I make a second consideration, where am I to go? Everything combined together, make me at times miserable beyond description. I have been given to understand that Penang, Singapore and Malacca are poor places for a person in my circumstances, all the situations being filled by those who have left Bencoolen before me, and as I have entered the Dutch Service, I am fearful John Company will allow me no claim on them, but tell me to look to my late Masters. I do not detail to you my woes in the hope of finding relief from you, as I have always received from your friends much more than I ever had a right to expect. I merely relate them to you as I know you will sympathise with me, sympathy is at all times pleasing to one in depressed feelings, but a father's sympathy is more pleasing than all, but enough of this - I will no longer distress you with so sad a relation of my prospects. I must hope for the best, and as I am yet very young and having lately learnt some little experience, I trust ere long something eligible may turn up, when I shall not fail to write and let you know my good fortune. Believe me to be My dear Father with kind love and regards to all at Bevis Hill,

Yours affect. Son,

Wm. G. Day.

P.S. Excuse this scrawl, and haste, as I have not time to say more.

Letter 14

Endorsed in another hand: from Wm. Day 25 July 1827

To: Mrs. Chas. Day, Bevis Hill, nr. Southampton, Hants.
Per Borneo, Wm. G. Day

Bencoolen,
25th July 1827

My dear Mrs. Day,

A long period has again elapsed since any intercourse has passed between us, and though I have been of late a tardy correspondent, yet in this instant I cannot accuse myself of being remiss in writing to you as I have written you several letters since I received your last communication. Whether you have forgotten to write or some miscarriage happens in the conveyance (as my father has also been silent for a long time) it is impossible for me to conjecture, tho' I am willing to attribute your silence to the latter cause, but situated as we are with obstacles at present, (and I'm fearful for ever) insuperable to any other intercourse than by letter, I think it unnecessary hardship that any circumstance should exist to interrupt our occasional or more frequent intercourse. What then are the obstacles? Pray let me know them.

Since my last letters to Bevis Hill, the contents of which I have no doubt my father has made you acquainted with, nothing has transpired with regard to myself either for the better or for the worse - matters are at a stand still. But as to the state of affairs in general I am sorry to say that the prospect is truly dismal. As to the Settlement there is not a hope of its ever being able to re-establish itself on its former respectable footing, but on the contrary, the progress of men is too plain, and quite inevitable. I have always said that I should remain at Bencoolen as long as circumstances would admit, matters are at last come to a crisis, and much to my regret, I am making preparations for my departure from poor Bencoolen. Bevis Hill has the first place in my heart and poor Bencoolen undoubtedly the second, like Bevis Hill, it has been a spot where I passed many many happy days, such as I have no right to expect, will ever pass again. Necessity has no law - and consequently I must leave. It is my intention to go to one of the eastern settlements and try to be employed by the Company, having been already employed by them I have some claim to their favorable considerations and having a few months back memorialized to the Supreme Govt. of Bengal praying for my arrears of Salary and to be readmitted into their service, I am in hopes that all I have prayed for will be complied with. In this case I shall exert my interest with some of my old friends to get me appointed to Malacca. I more particularly wish to go there as I understand that the soil and climate are both conducive to the cultivation of the Spice Tree and as I have gained some little experience at Bencoolen in that branch of Indian Agriculture, I am in hopes of being able to make use of it to my some advantage.

I have learnt by letters from Singapore that your brother Robert is in his usual health, and continues his usual dissipated life. What makes the case still more distressing to those interested in his welfare, is that I have also learnt that your friend Sir John Claridge, on his arrival at Penang made very particular enquiries of him, but finding him so out of the common habits of gentlemen in general, that has taken little further notice of him. I also understand that it is Robert's intention to accept of his pension (nearly £200) and going to Europe, he has not ever written me since he left this. I have however not forgotten him, and write him occasionally to remind him of those friends so much interested in his good, but I'm fearful all is labour lost, his habits have taken too deep a root and to eradicate them is an impossibility. Do not think my dear Mrs. D. that what I write of yr brother, is written by me through any splene that I may bear towards him. I am actuated from the best of motives, for I wish you to know the true state of your poor brother's affairs. He is no ones enemy but his own. His trip to Europe may be beneficial to him, as I understand that he labours under extreme depression of spirits, in such a case a change of scene may be wished for. Was it not for his pecuniary disharassments, his pension would be an ample subsistence in England.

I have given you a long account of yr brother and myself, it is now time to make some enquiry of how you and all the family at Bevis Hill are. There has been such an increase that I can no longer enumerate them and enquire separately of them. I however trust that they are all quite well and Charles & Robert now become fine young men. I more particularly think of them than of the rest, for what reason I do not know, but they are all equally dear to me. I often think of the pleasure of one day seeing some of them in India, but my Dr. Mrs. Day, never consent to any of them coming out to this country unless permanently fixed in the service. I would rather forego the pleasure of meeting them than they should have to put with the sufferings that every young man of a liberal education, not fixed in the Service, has daily to experience. Yr. poor brother is one instance, but not a solitary one for I myself had my share of regrets, and all others similarly situated undergo the same trial. Bear in mind this particular, and do not take it amiss that it has come from a person who can have no other interest at heart but the welfare of his dearest friends, and your family must ever be the first on that list.

My dear Miss Perreau,

I do not write you a letter, but you will not on this account conceive that you are less dear to me than the rest of the family at Bevis Hill or that I think the less of you. I should hope that you know yr place in my heart - you may tax me with tardyness but I hope never with ingratitude, the many kindnesses I have experienced from both you and Mrs. Day are still fresh in my memory and be assured that I am still to you both as well as to the rest of the family,

Yours ever affectionately,

Wm. G. Day.

P.S. Our worthy friend Mr. Baskett continues to enjoy his usual health and flow of good spirits, and I sincerely hope he may continue to do so for should anything happen to the old man under my present circumstances I should really be at a loss whom to look to as a friend, as to my father's friend Mr. Bogle I am sorry to say that any further friendship between us has subsided, as I have had a serious quarrel with him, he being averse to my living at my father's plantation at Combong, the result of my visit there has been attended to this quarrel, but so with much good to my father, as I have been able to get him such a produce as he never yet had since he left Bencoolen, this is the only good news that I have been able to communicate to him for these two years past. The next opportunity will bring him the fruits of this year's Clove harvest, somewhere abouts £250 to £300.

Letter 15

Endorsed from Wm. Day 28 July 1827

Bencoolen
28th July 1827

My Dear Father,

During the long space of a year and a half I have received but One solitary pledge of the existence of my friends at Bevis Hill. How this painful silence has occurred I am at a loss, even to hazard a conjecture, the dredful thought that you may be no more intruded itself on my mind, but was this the case, which God forbid, some of my kind friends would not be silent on such an event, and some tiding ere this, from some one or other would have reached me. What then can be the reason of this painful silence.? I have no doubt that my silence towards you must have been equally as painful, for I must admit, that of late my communications have not been so frequent, this has been owing to a wish not to remind you too often of my distresses.

My last letter dated so far back as Septr informed you of my unexpected dismissal from the Dutch service, since that period nothing material has transpired to make my circumstances either better or worse, with a little studious economy I have been able to keep out of debt, or I should more properly say, that I have not increased them. My present course of life is however far from being pleasant, living on ones witts is a poor pittance. I have therefore made .up my mind to go round to Singapore and try my luck once again with "Honorable John" for they are really good masters. I understand by letters from Penang that your friend Sir John Claridge has been making very particular enquiries respecting me and mentioned some intention of writing me an invitation to his place. I have not yet been so much favoured, but as all my friends from that quarter advised me so very strenuously to come round and see the judge, I think that by going round I shall loose nothing and have some chance of getting some something, and as I am at present idle, it will be no time lost, under these circumstances I shall be induced with great reluctance to leave poor Bencoolen. Baskett, Grant and myself have stood the brunt of the battle for some time, and I shall be truly sorry to leave them to the fate of our relentless enemies. We are the only three still remaining. Our friend B. also thinks of moving, and does not altogether like the idea of my leaving him, as he may require Grant's and my services. He has however consented to my going.

I now come to a most pleasing part of my communications to you. I am just come into town for a month, to pack up this seasons produce of Cloves. Your half share being 25 peculs. You are indebted for this produce to my having gone out and resided altogether at Combong, it has however been the cause of my quarreling with Bogle. The matter is this - A month previous to the Clove season I informed Bogle of my intention of going out to Combong to look after the produce as the appearance of the trees promised a very abundant harvest and that I thought it necessary for one of us to be on the spot at that time and told him that I supposed his Magisterial functions would not admit of his leaving Marlbro - the only reply was "Are you". Two days previous to my intention of going out, he sent his son to live at Combong as you may suppose as a check upon me. All very fair so far. I then proposed to Bogle a mess between his son and myself and proposed terms to him which were treated with much coolness and redicule, which gave rise to a letter from me to him on the subject, wherein (in the course of our correspondence) our mutual opinions were exchanged with some warmth. This matter as I thought , has passed, his son having managed to come to a better understanding with me than his father did. I was however mistaken, for Bogle continued to harp on this subject to Baskett and others and the course of the conversation always introduced subjects and matters which (as he thought every one would believe to be correct) were detrimental to my character. You must be aware that Bogle and myself are brother executors to Williams estate. B. having been the idle one and myself the active one - on this point he made many most unfriendly insinuations, so much so, that Baskett called upon me at Combong and related one such tale - that I immediately wrote to Bogle "that it was folly to continue to address him as hitherto, when his feelings were so much at variance with his expression (he always addressing me "Dr. William") I then informed him of what I had heard, he replied, in great length, to my note, in a very satirical style, I consequently called upon, at his own house, and taxed him with all that he had spoken of me - to which he made a most firm denial. You must know, that after replying to my note just alluded to, he went to Baskett and others and showing my note and boasting of the spirited answer he had given and said that he had given me a "settler", he was mistaken on this point, and afterwards expressed his surprise at my visit, he made many concessions which I could not accept, as the circumstances related to me by Baskett, I was certain, were true, and fear alone was the cause of his denial on the different subjects put to him, and his concessions originated from the source, for this reason I rejected them.

A short time after this affair, a chinaman on one of my plantations went to the Police office to complain against me for having given him half a dozen stripes with a horse whip. Bogle availed himself of this opportunity of giving me further annoyance, he went to the Acting Resident and laid the case before him, (a matter quite unnecessary), but as B. thought it would give the case a more "serious appearance". B. however wrote me to compromise the matter with the fellow, but at the same time told the chinaman to come to Court on the following Monday. I succeeded in making matters up with the man, which B. was not aware of, and as usual went about inviting the planters to come to his office on Monday and hear the case, as the Resident was determined to make an example of it, and that I was to be fined 500 Rupees. On coming into on Monday as customary, not to answer to the chinaman's prosecution I was assailed by every one upon this subject. I immediately went to Baskett and requested James Grant & Lewis to accompany me and they then came to a resolution of making a joint memorial to the Supreme Govt. should the sentence be enforced after which I called upon the Resident (a weakminded Dutchman) and informed him that I had been given to understand that he had given directions to the Magistrate to fine me in the sum of Rupees 500, and beg'd to be informed if such was the case, as I did not intend to resist the fine but on the contrary would at the present moment give him an order for the amount on Baskett but at the same time I should request my passport for Batavia and further made him acquainted of the resolution of the planters in case the law should be enforced, as the law had hither to allowed every planter to inflict one dozen lashes whereas I had only given half that number and I said to him that I thought he had allowed himself to be led away by what B. had told him, who had (as he was aware) feelings of animosity towards me, and further that it was evident such was the case as the sentence was fixed before the case had been heard, as B. had made it known to several. His brother in law who was then president, was one who had heard it and I taxed him with it, which he could not deny, the upshot of the business was that the Resident was happy to drop it and B. got a severe reprimand.

You must conceive that this widened the breach, B. continued to persecute me more than ever, on every occasion, and gave me much annoyance at Combong, by countermanding my orders on the plantation etc., none of which I ever allowed to be attended to, as my being on the spot constitutes me master, and which I told him, after much litigation too long for me to enter into, suffice it to tell you that I was again obliged to make a personal call at his house on the matter of Cooley line at Combong. Bogle wished to bring his extra hands in the plantation as Coolies and some difference in the charges being disputed as also to the number of his own peoples actually at work we came to higher words than ever. I told him that I was not afraid to make my assertions to his face and wished that he had the spirit to do so to mine, he replied "I will now do it !!!!!" and actually brought forward the whole of the unfriendly insinuations and assertions, which Baskett had related to me, and which he had so firmly denied on a former occasion. I was so annoyed and hurt that I gave him the "lie", he attempted to use compulsory measures to make me leave his house. I told him that if he laid his hands on me I would that moment knock him down and which I should have done, had he called any force to turn me out, he got very agitated and allowed me to leave his house without further molestation, thus have matters been with your old friend Bob Bogle and myself, he has endeavoured to instil in every ones mind that our quarrel originated in some misunderstanding regarding William's estate, that was, truly, a secondary cause, my <u>going out to Combong</u> was the sole and <u>principal</u> one, I have related thus fully my quarrel as I should wish you to know the unfriendly part that B. has acted towards me, and all on account of my wish to see that justice should be done to yourself for on my first going out I candidly told him that I wished to ascertain the actual produce of <u>One Season</u> of Cloves. A point now ascertained beyond any further doubt.

The account B. gave of the former season (which was considered <u>almost, tho' not quite</u> so plentiful as the present) was that he got <u>barely 30 peculs</u>. I have however managed to get good <u>50 peculs</u> somewhere near upon 40 pr cent better, from this circumstance you may be able to judge how far B. has done you justice; the Clove trees at Combong are getting very old and consequently diminish in their produce, the second, third, fourth and fifth crops are generally considered the most plentiful, after which they fall off. B. has reaped the whole of these harvests of which you have had no share and it is only at this period that you commence to get some returns for the large capital layed out on the plantation, had you always had such remittances as I have made as per accompanying Account Current, I should suppose that the property must have paid itself 5 or 6 times over, it was the fear of my ascertaining these points that induced him to throw obstacles in the way of my going out to live on the spot, and not succeeding in this point, he knew that when I had ascertained such low deceats that I should require an explanation and that we must ultimately quarrel, and William's estate he thought was a fair pretext for one.

What gives me great annoyance is Bogles continuing to persecute in every point he possibly can fix upon and is at this present moment bantering with some people under my charge instigating them to lodge a complaint against me for reducing their rice a thing that he has done himself on all his plantations. You cannot suppose to yourself what a villain I have to deal with, he is conscious that his bench protects him and that I am thereby prevented from inflicting the chastisement he so richly deserves. When an opportunity offers he may depend upon my calling him to a still severer account than the last. I told him so to his face, at first he thought to bully me, but he was grossly deceived.

Aug. 1st. After so much has been said respecting my quarrel, it is now time to say something respecting the plantation. The produce at the present moment is lower than I ever did know it, not more than 300 nuts a day (between us) this is however owing to length of dry weather not experienced for many years past - as the rains set in next month, a rise may be reasonably expected. The young plantation planted out by Bogle is coming up, but the better part of the trees have been injured by buffaloes, with a little care something may still be made of it and in three years more some return may be expected. I am waiting for the rains before I replace all the injured trees in the young Plantation. Respecting the labourers you will perceive by the enclosed list at the back of the Account Current that they are in number 19, and the extra hands included in the monthly abstract, belong to Bogle. It is necessary to have full as many as the abstract shews to keep the plantation in order. I have however from this month (there being no more cloves) allowed B. to take off 5 or 6 of his own people, with a view of reducing the expences which will after this month be considerably reduced. If possible I will do away with the Jemtooliss[39] or at least reduce his wages and with a few other alterations I expected to reduce the expences One third. What makes the expences so high is the Bengal rice at R's 10 per bag, whereas the country rice may be procured at half that price, but then I have no funds, and have been obliged to take rice upon credit from Mr. William's estate, the rice is by far the heaviest charge against the plantation if you can only put me in funds in that commodity to order it down from Calcutta, tho' what with freight etc., it will fall very short of R's10 by the time it reached me at Bencoolen. As to yr letting me draw on your agents for cash, this matter is not practicable as no one wants bills as a remittance, for not a planter has sufficient cash to pay his monthly establishment. The rice supplied to Combong has been paid by me by a bill on my agents in Calcutta. I hardly know what to advise on this matter. One way would be to get cash down from Batavia or Padang, for we are obliged to send bills to those places to be cashed for we have no money in the place, not even copper cash, you must suppose, that under these circumstances, what disadvantages we have to incur.

Baskett is two months in arrears with the whole of his establishment and stands indebted to the Government upwards of Rs.10,000, for duties on his Opium and piece goods, when B. is pushed to such expences what must others be.

You will perceive in our Account that I have charged you for half share of a smoaking house which I built at Botany Bay, this has been a mutual benefit, if you however object to participate in the expence, strike it out and any other parts of the accounts or charges that you may consider in the same light, you can also strike off. I will be candid with you. I have made the same charges that I make to my other constituents and have made no difference towards you, and my charges I will allow are not altogether low. You may from this judge how far the plantation with a little rain, could or could not pay for itself. The balance in my favor may be paid to Messrs. Robt. Scott & Co., Broad St., Buildings, these gentlemen are agents for several of my constituents and have accounts with me. I intend making them a remittance (my first), by the same opportunity will take your Cloves and spices I have now on hand, but when that will be I cannot say or by what route I cannot say, but more than probable via Singapore. You may expect to receive by this remittance 20 (twenty) peculs of Cloves and about 5 peculs in Nutmegs or mace this remittance should realise you, net proceeds, somewhere upon £350 to £370 and what with the other remittances which you must ere this have realised I should calculate upon the whole that you must have got nearly upon £500 altogether. I suppose this is much more than what you have ever been able to get out of Bogle.

Respecting the men it is my intention to send the whole of B's own people away and substitute them with Meneering debtors[40] for small amounts - for. B.. considers that he has a superiority over me on this account and is continually taking them off on his own business, such as carting his rice out of town, cutting firewood etc., on the plea of their being his own people, altho' they get rice, belangio[41] and clothing from you, to prevent this I shall adopt the above place, he talks of taking away the whole flock of cattle, and leave only 13 head as the flock belonging to Combong, he has not yet done it, but when he does some enquiry must be made respecting them. If he does take them away we must purchase others, for Combong being an old plantation manure is the most essential point to be looked to, a want of that and there will be a great want of produce. Cattle are at present moment dirt cheap 7 & 8 dollars a head whereas in former times they were 25 to 27 per head, under these circumstances it would be folly not to attend to this essential point.

Let me have a list of the slaves you left here both at Combong and Botany Bay - and also let me know whether in any of Bogle's accounts he has given you credit for Dollars 100 (one hundred) on acct. of amt. purchase of See Roumin, a woman whom you must recollect he used her so ill that she was emancipated by the Court under the idea that she was Bogle's own slave, if otherwise he was to be fined R's 1000. I hold the original certificate of the woman's freedom, which I found amongst the late Mr William's papers, wherein he certifies that "See Roumin my own Slave" "he hereby emancipates". She could not have been at that time his slave as he must have first written for your permission to purchase, but to save the 1000 rupees he drew out the paper alluded to - let me hear all that you know on this subject - if he has not credited you for her amount purchase, say so, and I'll get it out of him, for he has repeatedly told me that he had paid that amount on her account.

As to little Botany Bay I cannot speak too highly in its praises, even in these times - it still continues to supply me with my curry & rice and when the younger trees planted out in the place of those cut down, come into bearing I may expect nearly double the produce. I can safely say that there is not another plantation in the place that gives so handsome a produce. I shall be very sorry to leave it, but it will be in very good hands, and as there is a flock of cattle upon it, there will be no want of manure. I do not think it can altogether go to ruin, but on the contrary, under all circumstances, even if spices were to fall to Dr. 50 per pecul, still it would more than pay the expences, but few plantations can say as much. My plan when I leave will be to remit the whole of the produce to England and remit from my pay, such sums as may be required for its expences, for I have been given to understand from good authority that I may expect Rs 200 a month out of this I can save a third. You see that I am all on the saving system, the transfer has taught me a lesson. I have now felt the want of cash most bitterly, it is too true. Misfortunes are chastening.

I must now let you know what are my reasons pro & con for going round to Singapore. I am really like the Jack-ass between two thistles, and know not which one to eat or which one to go to. The case stands as thus. With respect to the inducements for my remaining at Bencoolen, they are many. The few British Inhabitants (and truly speaking there are only 4 or 5 respectable ones) now residing here make it necessary for 2 or 3 to be fixed to look after the plantations and property left by those gone away, hitherto I have been generally selected by those gone away, and I can safely assert that no other Englishman has more extensive agencies to transact than myself. Not even old Baskett. I have 13 plantations under my charge and consequently near upon 3 to 400 people under my superintendence. At one time I had almost double that establishment under my charge, being in charge of Wm. Lewis affairs, the most extensive planter and merchant at this place. He took his nephew with him to Singapore, but failing in his expectations, was obliged to send him back to look after his property, since which I have only One third of the plantation whereas before this I had better than one half of Bencoolen under my management. You must suppose that in all this business of agencies there are many pickings. Commission etc.

Another most urgent reason, but bear in mind this I could only avow to you and no one else, so let it be to yourself. Poor old Baskett has taken a strong partiality to James Grant and myself and by what I know of his affairs that I am induced to suppose that we two will in a great measure, in the case of the old gentleman's death, replace the two Lewis'. I do not suppose so, for James Grant drew out the old man's Will and was desired to make the contents known to me, the old man is however much involved in Calcutta, but has some firms in England, he will not die worth much property, but I understand that he intends making over previous to his departure what property he intends should fall to us - with view of avoiding the duties on "Colateral Succession" and other litigations. Should however any renumeration be given by the British Govt. there is no knowing but that under all these circumstances I might again visit Bevis Hill. I have often been at a loss to find out how the old gentleman took such a liking for me. I knew nothing of the matter further than he one day beg'd that I would be one of his executors, and a few days afterwards he drew out his will and I learnt from James Grant a most unexpected tale. You must bear in mind to keep this letter from the sight of any one, and never broach the subject to H.R. Lewis for he would go mad did he dream of such a thing, for he has an idea that he is heir to everything, but he will be much mistaken'd. He will however have no occasion to complain, as he is not altogether struck out, he will no longer hold a principal part in the play, but nevertheless he will hold a second rate one.

I alluded in a former part of my letter to Mr. B's reluctance in allowing me to leave, as it is his intention to leave this as soon as he can bring his concerns to a focus, as he would wish me to be here to look after his property. In this state of my affairs it will not be altogether certain that I take up my residence to the eastward, there must be very strong inducements indeed. Nothing under 200 rupees a month will operate to that effect. My principal inducement indeed is to draw my arrears of salary as many others have done on the plea of re-entering the Service, which will put about 3,000 rupees in my pocket and it will give me an opportunity of looking about me. I shall set myself down at the place I am appointed to for 5 or 6 months, and then request leave of absence to settle my affairs at Bencoolen, which if they refuse I can very gravely say that so urgent are my affairs that I am reluctantly obliged to resign the Service. Baskett says that his departure will not be for this next year to come and that there will be full time for me to go round and try my luck, he says that nothing but 300 R's per month should operate as an inducement to my leaving this place. For truly speaking I have all my comforts about me, such as I shall not get elsewhere for the next ten years to come. I begun to be known to the natives, and should any change take place in the politics of Europe which would effect the politics of the east, I may fairly conclude that some change would be for the better.

I have let you into this secret of my intimacy with Mr. B. as it was absolutely necessary for you to know this to enable you in some way to account for my intentions but on no account let this matter go further. Don't hint such a thing to H.R. Lewis, for he would not scruple to argue the point with the old man, on the right of his disinheritance. So consumate is his impudence. Not keeping his secrets to himself has the principal cause of Mr. B's dislike towards him, as he boasts of the man's favorable intentions towards him. Let him remain in a happy state of ignorance on this matter. I am inclined to think that he has some fears on this point for both him and his brother have done their utmost to persuade both Grant and myself to leave the place, fearful that we are undermining them. I have never attempted such a thing, for Mr. B's favorable inclinations towards me were quite unexpected but since I have gained his esteem I shall do my best not to forfeit it.

I have been given to understand that Robert Perreau continues to be the same strange character, he has thwarted all Sir John Claridge's good intentions towards him, it is really distressing to hear such repeated unpleasant accounts. Mr. Winter, my former partner at Benturing writes me that his mind is quite gone, he has however his lucide intermissions, he fancies himself haunted by a Bengalees Convict and no reasoning can persuade him to the contrary. Some of his friends have persuaded him to accept of his pension and go to Europe which would with a little economy and in other hands than his own (for he requires to be treated like a child) would be sufficient to make him comfortable without being a burthen to his friends, he talks of taking with him to Europe (for he actually intends attempting this out of the way scheme) two big hulking sons who know not either to read or write. I have written to Winter begging him to prevent his going away before I come round, and on no account to allow him to be so foolish as to take his sons, but Robert is so strange that any opposition would only strengthen his resolution of taking them. I have written him repeatedly but not a line have I received from him. I have written the ladies on this subject but no so fully as I have done to you. However, use your own discretion respecting this part of my letter. It may or it may not be as well to let them know the true state of poor Robert's mind.

By the bye, it had almost escaped me to inform you that in my absence James Grant will be my Attorney and should you require any information respecting your affairs in this respect, to make your communications to him - Combong will be put under him, for Baskett is getting too old and too many cares on his mind to give the necessary attention, in fact, James Grant and Baskett are two people in one, for Grant lives in the country at a very extensive young plantation planted out on the old woodlands plantation, which plantation is the joint property of Grant & Baskett. Mr. Baskett has of late been complaining of a pain on his chest and I am sorry to say, at times, does not enjoy his usual good spirits. The transfer has been a serious matter to us all, but more particularly to him, for had it not taken place, he would ere this have been in England enjoying himself, living upon the revenue of his property at this place, whereas at present moment it will barely pay its own expences. This Clove season has however set a little on his legs again, his young plantation having borne for the first time, from which he reaped 100 peculs!

I must now make some enquiries of how you have been since our last intercourse. I hope you enjoy good health and that you may continue to do so is my constant hope and wish. Charles and Robert I presume are now fine young men and I trust the rest of the family promise to be the same. Often do I contemplate the pleasure of meeting some part of them at a future period in India, but I should hope to see them come out with Writers covenants, for India is strangely altered since your time. A young man let his education have been ever so liberal or his connextions ever so good, if not in the Service (as it is term'd) little or in fact no notice is taken of him, he is looked upon as an inferior sort of being. I have advised Mrs. Day on this subject, you must not take it amiss for I can have no other motive at heart than their welfare and happiness. India is but a poor field for an adventurer. One must come out with the security of a fortune, as to looking for one, it is a much easier matter to do so in Europe than in India.

I must also make enquires of all my old friends. How is John Edward? and where is he? he has not proved himself to be the sterling character that I at one time took him to be. I have only received one pledge of the existence of our former friendships, and that one was a lame apology for his neglect, but begging me not to write until I heard from him again as he was uncertain as to his destination, this was a poor subterfuge to save postage, he might have said so to me, for at one time I knew the very innermost feelings of his heart. Time however works strange changes. How is my old friend Capt. Fiott and the rest of his family. The Bullens I have not forgotten. I see by some papers that Captn. B. had gone out Commodore of the African Station, this was however some time back. The Minchims are also old friends. I hope also that they are all well and hearty, remember me to them all, and tell old Minchim to remember me to Fred. Minchim when he writes to him, if I knew where to address him I would give him a line for "Friendship" sake and days of Aulde Lang syne. I am getting at the bottom of my third sheet of paper which warns me to draw my epistle to a conclusion. I must consequently conclude for my hand is tired, and be assured that it is with my heart Your's very dutifully and affectionately,

Wm. G. Day.

To Charles Day, Esquire

Letter 16

Stamped: India Letter Plymouth
Also in another hand from Wm. Day 20th Novr. 1827

To: Charles Day Esqre, Bevis Hill, Southampton,
Hants.
Per Matilda, Singapore 20th Novr. Wm. G. Day.

Singapore
20th Novr. 1827

My Dear Father,

The purport of my present letter is merely to advise you of my having left Bencoolen about 2 months ago. On my way to this place I touched at Batavia and was much pleased at having made a visit there, for I met with much attention from several of the British merchants. My stay was not sufficiently long to enable me to form an opinion altogether of the place, but by what I have seen of both this place and Batavia I am induced to return to my old quarters. Bencoolen notwithstanding all her lost beauty still has charms for me. On my arrival (10 or 11 days ago) I found your old friend John Prince on the point of giving over charge of the Settlement, preparatory to his return to old England, in justice to him I must say that he offered to do all that lay in his power, but it is so very limited, that there was nothing proposed in any way worthy of my notice. All that I could have expected would have been a paltry 100 R's per month out of which I must have paid from 40 to 50 R's on acc't of house rent.

On leaving Bencoolen I expected to have chum'd up with my old partner Mr. Winter, but unfortunately I found on my landing that he had, like many others, gone to that bourne from whence no travellor returns, he had, poor fellow, written me many pressing invitations to come round and spend a few months with him, this was the principal inducement for my quiting the coast, as it was my intention to have accepted of the 100's R's per month, and ultimately to apply for my arrears of salary, which I could not do without having previously established myself as a settler in the place, not foreseeing Winter's death I had come round with nothing more than a trunk of clothes (having disposed of such property as would realise anything like a price to enable me to defray my passage) trusting that living in another man's house, furniture and other household necessaries would not be required, a box of clothes was all my store, consequently did I remain, the expence to recommence housekeeping would soon run away with the arrears and as my good friend Mr. Baskett gave me to understand that it was his anxious wish that I should not leave Bencoolen, as he was only awaiting my return to leave the place, under all circumstances, I have made up my mind to return to the West Coast, trusting that some better luck may await me there.

I have further to advise you that I have placed, under the care of Messrs Gutherie & Clark & Co., 20 cases of Cloves, each case containing one pecul & 2 cases of Spice, One containing Nutmegs weighing lbs 370 & one Mace wg. lbs 157 with directions to them to forward the spice with the least possible delay to Messrs Morris & Renny, London. Freight was not procurable by the present opportunity, there is however a vessel now laying in the roads wanting freight for Europe, it is expected that she will sail in a month or six weeks. You may expect to receive the above quoted spices by that opportunity. I shall advise with Messrs Morris & Renny on the subject, and beg of them to await your instructions respecting them.

I left your share of Combong under the care of our friend Mr. Baskett, as also the produce on hand, and with the produce collected during my absence (as it was getting up when I left) I hope to be able to make you a still further remittance, for the vessel on which I go round to the West Coast touches at Bencoolen for freight, and returns to this place. I shall let have all the freight I can scrape together, as it is only on these conditions she takes me round, paying at the same time R's 1000 for my passage to say from Bencoolen and back again - as I go on in the same vessel that brought me here. We touch on our way round at Malacca, Palo Penang, Padang, Pogie Island & Bencoolen. I shall then have gone round Sumatra, and can say that I have seen something of the coast. I however pay pretty high for my excursion and did the vessel go direct I might have expected a cheaper passage, but as she is going on a trading voyage and will not reach Bencoolen for 2 months I am in consequence obliged to pay somewhat higher. I calculate upon being away altogether from Bencoolen about four months, travelling about for that time at £1000 is not very exorbitant. I however can ill afford it. With kind regards to all at Bevis Hill,

Believe me to be

Yours very dutifully and affectionately

Wm. G. Day.

P.S. By the bye yr last letters are dated Dcr 1825, what are the reasons for this silence?

Included with William's letter of 20 Nov 1827

Endorsed: from Wm. Day dated 20 Novr. 1827 rec'd May 1828
Advising of a consignment of spices to Morris & Renny

To Charles Day Esq., Southampton

Dear Sir,

No.11 20 C.D	) I have to advise you that Messrs Gutherie & Clark of this place have
Cloves	) received my directions to transmit to the address of yr Agents in
No.1 Ditto	) London Twenty two cases of Spice as marked & numbered in the
lbs 370	) margin, and have to request that you will communicate to Messrs
No.1 Mace C.D.	) Morris & Renny your wishes respecting the disposal of the same, as I
lbs 157	) have advised with those Gentlemen to await your instructions on that subject.

I remain,

Dear Sir,

Yours faithfully

Wm.G. Day.

Singapore
20th Novr. 1827

Endorsed: From Wm. Day at Bencoolen dated 31st May 1828 enclosing abstract of all expences & produce of Combong Plantation.
Answered 16 April 1829
Sent up to H. Lewis to be forwarded to Bencoolen.

Bencoolen 31st May 1828

To Charles Day Esqre., Southampton.

Dear Sir,

Enclosed I have the pleasure to forward you our Account Current up to this date and shewing balance in my favor of £2385. 15. 4 which I trust may be found correct and satisfactory.

With respect to the enclosed I beg to observe that no commission on produce forwarded, or charge for superintendence, has yet been made; these points having been left to your consideration. Should however the balance be found satisfactory, and any addition allowed for superintendence etc., The amo't I should feel obliged by your placing into the hands of my Agents Messrs Robt. Scott & Co. London.

With warmest assurances of my lively attentions to your interest here,

I remain,

Dear Sir,

Yours faithfully,
Wm. G. Day.

Letter 17

Endorsed: From William Day Bencoolen dated 31st May 1828
Answd. 16 April 1829. Sent up to H Lewis to be forwarded.
Stamped India Letter Portsmouth and 'Forwarded by your Obdt.
Srvt. H.L. Johnston & Co., Singapore'.
Bishop Mark G.20 Mar. 1829.

To Charles Day, Esqre., Bevis Hill, near Southampton, Hants
To care of Messrs Ladbrooke & Co., Cornhill, London.

Bencoolen 31st May 1828

My Dear Father,

I wrote you in December last dated Singapore acquainting you of the reasons for my leaving Bencoolen and making a visit to the former place and my intentions of proceeding to Malacca and Penang. At the latter place I had the honor of a most pressing invitation from your friends the Claridges to take up my quarters with them during my stay there and received from them the most flattering attentions. Sir John made me every offer of his Services and I am confident they are made with sincerity, but as I perceived that his quarrel with the Governor had greatly diminished his patronage as well as in some measure, had tied his hands, I prefered rather to return for the present, and await the result of this business. Rumour seems to say that one of the two must be removed. The general wish is that it may be the Governor for he is morose in his manner and in mind illiberal in the extreme. The truth of the matter is this, Mr. Fullerton is envious of Sir John, as he takes away from him a great deal of his patronage, and equally as much of his consequence both galling to a "barra Saib". I write you that fully as I know it will be interesting to the Scotts to learn the true state of things. As to the feelings of the settlers they are undoubtedly in favour of Sir John, tho' at Penang they dare not say so, but at

Singapore, they are more independent and speak out more freely and by what I could learn there, some of the Merchants hint something about petitioning the Govt' not to remove Sir John. Let the Scotts hear of this.

I have written you enclosing our Account Current addressing the letter to the care of your Agents. In it I have said nothing relating to Combong fearful that I should not have time, but the vessel being detained it gives me an opportunity of saying what I wished. I wrote you from Singapore and forwarded at the same time the last season's crop of Cloves and some Nutmegs and Mace. On my leaving this I ordered the produce to be taken to Mr. Baskett that is to say from the 1 Novr. 27 to 31st March 28 during the first 3 months of which time every plantation gave a most extraordinary produce, Combong gave from 3500 to 4000 nuts for 2 months following, in this case Mr. B has a large produce on hand. The produce with me is merely for April and May during which time it has not averaged from 3 to 400 a day. The trees however look very promissing being full of young fruit, the only fear is that the dry weather may sett in before the fruit is well sett, if so, we shall loose half of it. We will hope for the best. You will observe by the Acct. Current forwarded to you that the expences of Combong during the time I was away have been paid by me. Mr. B having debited me with a share tho' he kept the produce in his own hands, which he does not intend remitting, until you acknowledge his former remittance in a Set of Bills per Borneo. His keeping the produce and my bearing the expences comes hard upon me considering the present balance in my favor, for had I the produce I would take it at the market price & remit on my account and thereby save Interest of money. You will also observe that a part of that balance has been to your debit for the last year and upwards for it includes expences since I had charge of Combong & further that I have made no charge for Superintendence nor have I had credit for commission on produce 5 per ct. as allowed by other constituents, all these points I leave to yourself. I can only say the smallest donation will be most thankfully received.

It is my intention this month to make still further reductions in the expences. I intend to dispense with the Jantooliss, cattle keeper & Gourdan and substitute them with our own people on the plantation - and other reductions if possible.

Should it be my intention to continue at Bencoolen, which is more than probable, owing to Baskett's going away and leaving James Grant and myself his agents as well as his business & good name. I then expect a much better opening. than at present, altho' my present business as Agent for Several individuals is far from being unworthy of my consideration, under these circumstances I find a great inconvenience and loss to myself for want of credit at Calcutta. May I enlist your assistance in this business, either by a letter of recomendation to your Agents or a credit on your own funds in their hands say to the amount of Fifteen or twenty thousand rupees. I should however prefer the former place, as it would be at no risk to yourself. I would however free you from any risk on the other hand by Insuring my life for the amount of the credit making the same in your favor. I would not solicit this did I not think that something might be done with such credit, for it is not improbable that Grant and myself may be (after Baskett leaves) connected in business, but without bringing in equal funds with him, this cannot take place. At present I am obliged to sell the whole of produce of all my plantation (I mean those under my charge) to Mr. Baskett at Ps 60 a coppee - equal to 53-55 silver to meet my monthly expences, and Mr. B. remits his money in this way, he not only remits his money but turns full 10 pr. cent by the remittance, this alone would be to me a handsome profit, for thus had I credit in Calcutta and commissioned goods from there so as to put me on ready cash here, and by that means remit the produce (now sold to B.) on my own account and not saying anything of the profits on the sale of the goods, I might under these circumstances make something well worthy of my attention. I would not project such a plan did I not think something might be made by it, think of it and see what can be done.

To give you an idea of how I stand at present in the settlement, I need only tell you that I have 10 (ten) plantations under my charge, four of which give me Ps 200 per month, in fact, I make a charge of Ps 50 per month Superintendence, besides a commission of 5 pr. cent on all sales by which I calculate that my present monthly income amounts from 300 to 350 rupees pr month from which I have been able to pay all my debts & save a little money in the bargain. I think I may with every justice say that I am the only person in the settlement saving money. These are urgent reasons for my sticking close to Bencoolen, for I find that someone must remain there and take care of the property of those who leave it. Baskett will be gone in about 2 months more and then I may expect a very considerable increase in business as well as income. Such news I know must be pleasing to you, but I assure you my earnings are dearly bought at the expence of loss of friends, society and everything that makes life indurable. Only picture to yourself poor Bencoolen reduced to the very last stages of ruin with 3 or 4 European inhabitants, when I say Europeans I mean English, for the Dutch do not deserve the name of a civilized people for they are less civilized than the natives themselves.

Under these circumstances you will not say that I misapply the word when I say that I am unhappy and what has tended to make me more so is, the silence. with which you have behaved towards me for the last 3 years. If you wish to hurt my feelings you have taken the most effectual way to do it. You may continue silent, but I shall not, or cannot, forget my duty towards you, and shall ever continue to write to you and let you know of my welfare, but you, My dear Sir, have already done more than I ever ought to have expected and consequently I cannot ask more of you, but if you would only now & then (I do not ask you to write as you used to do every 3 months) write me a few lines I do assure you that your letters would be welcome indeed. With kindest regards to yourself and all friends at Bevis Hill and remember me to enquiring friends

I remain,
Yrs. very affectionately,

dutifully,

Wm. G. Day.

To Charles Day Esqre,
Southampton.

P.S. Pray what is Robert Perreau a doing for no one has heard of him since he left Singapore. H.R. Lewis writes out that he came in for property amounting to £500 a year, if so, he is a lucky fellow. Tell him that Beasley has been obliged to accept his pension and go to Europe, that Pattallo is married as also Wm.T. Lewis, the former to Dr. Hares daughter and the latter to a Mallaca born lady of Dutch extraction.

Notes

1 Charles Day's manservant.

2 It could take anything up to 9 months for a letter to arrive from England.

3 'old Perreau' here refers to Robert Samuel Perreau, father of Charles Day's wife, Francis Mary Perreau. Robert Samuel Perreau was appointed Writer at Fort Marlborough on 24th January 1777. He eventually held a number of senior posts including those of Secretary to the Government and later First Assistant to the Resident and Magistrate. He died at Fort Marlborough on 22nd May 1811.

4 From the Malay ,"kabun" a garden.

5 Robert Bogle was the owner of the Mount Argyle spice plantation which his father JVLE Bogle, who died in 1824, set with nutmeg and clove plants in 1803 when the second shipment of spices from Amboina reached the settlement. Robert Bogle remained on after the British withdrawal in 1825 and died there in 1848.

6 Sir Thomas Stamford Raffles, Lieutenant Governor of Bencoolen at this time.

7 The Spanish dollar or piaster valued at five shillings (25p) was the trading dollar of the Far East.

8 Negro slaves from Madagascar were employed at Bencoolen from the earliest times. In 1766 there were 576 slaves at Fort Marlborough and the subordinate Residencies and by 1778 this number had increased to 1121. It was not until 1818 that Raffles started to free slaves.

9 John Prince, born on 1 April 1770, was the son of Captain John and Elizabeth Prince. He was appointed writer for Fort Marlborough in 1786 and held several posts of importance in Bencoolen and outlying Residencies. He succeeded Raffles as superintending officer in charge at Bencoolen during the transfer of the British west coast establishments to the Dutch in 1825. He later served as Resident Councillor at Singapore.

10 Opium was imported into Fort Marlborough from British India in increasing quantities during the eighteenth century. Some of it was consumed locally but much of it was used for financing the rapidly increasing tea trade with China. A chest of opium sold on average for 300 dollars but when scarce could fetch 3000 dollars.

11 William Baskett was the Tavern Keeper at Bencoolen. He had previously controlled the Company's opium farm there until Raffles had abolished it on assuming control of the Fort Marlborough Government in 1818. Baskett was apparently W T Lewis's (see below) agent and was involved in various shady deals, including the smuggling of slaves into Bencoolen from

Pulau Nias, an island further up the coast noted as a haunt for pirates.

12 William Thomas Lewis was born at Bencoolen. His father was a Lieutenant of Artillery in the Company's military service; his mother was Indonesian. He apparently went to sea for he arrived back at Fort Marlborough as a Midshipman in the Perseverance in 1806, but remained in the settlement after the ship sailed to China. His mother who lived at Bencoolen until 1820 apparently gave birth to two sons, Henry Robert, the eldest and Charles Richard, who was Assistant in the Magistrate's Office in 1820. WT Lewis transferred to the Strait's Settlement in 1825 and ultimately retired as Resident Councillor of Penang in 1860 after a total of 50 years service with the two governments.

13 Frances Keble Perreau was an Aunt of Charles Day by marriage, and sister to Robert Samuel Perreau.

14 Charles Day had thirteen further children by his marriage to Frances Mary Perreau.

15 Almost certainly malaria.

16 Dr Bell was Sir Stamford's personal surgeon. He returned with Raffles to England in April 1824.

17 George John Siddons, appointed a Writer to Bengal in 1803. He transferred to Fort Marlborough in 1808 and held various posts before being appointed Resident in December 1816. Raffles ousted him in March 1818 when he returned to Calcutta and became First Deputy to the Collector of Government Customs and Town Duties. He retired in 1838. The well known actress, Sarah Siddons, was George's mother.

18 James Grant was a contemporary of Thomas and William.

19 Robert Perreau was the son of Robert Samuel Perreau by his first wife, Mary Cooper (1768-1798), daughter of George Cooper, Surgeon of Gravesend, and his wife, Elizabeth. He was therefore a brother of Frances Mary Perreau, who married Charles Day in 1812.

20 A sicca rupee was worth about two shillings and fourpence, approximately 12p.

21 Before the introduction of Penny Postage in 1840, postage was paid by the recipient and not the sender.

22 Title of the son of a Javanese ruler.

23 A pecul equalled 136 lb wt.

24 The Dutch guilder or florin of 20 stivers was worth one shilling and ten pence, approximately 9p.

25 Thus.

26 Elder son of Robert Samuel Perreau (1760-1811) by his second marriage to Elizabeth Braham, nee Salmon.

27 Writing and copying out reports would be one of the main tasks of a Writer on the Company's establishment.

28 Thus.
29 "Apa boleh buat", Malay for "What can one do?".
30 A 'Godess' was the local term used for a young virgin, from the Indonesian word 'gades'.
31 George Canning, Chairman of the Board of EICo.,Foreign Secretary from 1822-1827 and subsequently Prime Minister for a short time.
32 Captain William Gordon Mackenzie of the 24th Native Industry, born 9 May 1785. Arrived in India as a Cadet in 1800. Took part at the capture of Cape of Good Hope in 1806 and Amboina in 1810. In Oct 1817 he was Second Assistant to Resident at Fort Marlborough and served as Resident of Malacca in 1825-26. Ill health prevented him from succeeding Raffles at Bencoolen.
33 This probably means £.
34 Lord Amherst, Governor General of India, (1823-1826).
35 Lord Moira, Marquess of Hastings, Governor General of India (1817-1813).
36 Coffrees were descendants of slaves originally imported from Mozambique and Madagascar.
37 Attendants.
38 30-40 bamboos of wet cloves equalled one pecul.
39 Record keeper, from the Malay 'tulis' to write.
40 Slave debtors.
41 Wages

Letter from Robert Samuel Perreau to his daughters, Eliza Henrietta and Francis Mary Perreau, July 1810.

Notes on letter from Robert Samuel Perreau to his daughters, Eliza Henrietta and Francis Mary Perreau, July 1810.

It would appear from this letter that Robert Samuel Perreau's daughters, Eliza Henrietta and Frances Mary, were about to embark on a journey to Calcutta, no doubt in the hope of finding suitable husbands. In so doing they transferred from the 'protection' of their unmarried aunt in England, Frances Keble Perreau, sister of Robert Samuel, to that of their aunt Elizabeth, wife of Duncan Campbell and sister to Mary, Robert Samuel's wife. Duncan Campbell was a Factor for the Company in Calcutta. Frances Mary, who subsequently married Charles Day, was eighteen years old at the time and Eliza Henrietta twenty two.

Whether this letter was giving them a father's permission to travel to India, or acknowledging a 'fait accompli', (as it is quite possible the letter might not have arrived until after they had left England), is not known. In any event Robert Samuel was in no position to do anything about it because he was in effect banished to Bencoolen on account of the debts he had run up in Calcutta, (see Introduction).

It is highly probable that Charles Day met his future wife in Calcutta, because he was transferred to Fort St. George (Madras) in 1807 and was senior Assistant there until 1811. During this time it is most likely he visited Calcutta because in September 1810 he had to repay money into the Bengal Treasury amounting to 45,000 Rs (about £5400)! He had, of course, known Robert Samuel in Bencoolen and therefore had the ideal introduction to the Perreau sisters.

The children that Robert Samuel refers to in his letter, apart from his son Robert, were by his second marriage to Elizabeth, nee Salmon, widow of John Braham. John Braham and his brother Philip were born at Bencoolen of European parents. They both held senior positions in the Fort Marlborough establishment and because of their local birth and intimate knowledge of Indonesian society were a force to be reckoned with in the dubious commercial environment of the region. John died in 1802. His wife, one of the few European women at Fort Marlborough, was described as 'young, accomplished, handsome and agreeable'. Robert Samuel died at Bencoolen the year after this letter, on 22 May 1811, aged 50.

Fort Marlbro' 17th July 1810
My Dear Girls

By the arrival of the Ocean on the 15th June, I had the satisfaction to receive a letter from each of you, and I would have answered them separately, as I should have done, till the interference of public business at the close of the dispatches, has brought me to the period where Mr Parry our late Resident, has actually embarked and the Ship expected to sail this Evening. - I nevertheless deem it proper, both to acknowledge your letters, which communicate the death of my much respected parent, and as it has produced a determination on your part to attach yourselves to the Sister of your dear Mother, and to place yourselves under her protection, to express my concurrence therein; - because, it shall not be said, that I will sacrifice my Children to any selfish considerations of my own, and as you have thought proper to make your choice, of the two alternatives placed before you, it is with confident satisfaction, I express the happiness I feel in your having so amiable and worthy a patroness as your Aunt Campbell. My original sentiments, however, are by no means altered by any arguments I have heard, and what those are, your Aunt Fanny is aware of. I yield them nevertheless, and I pray God that he will protect you both during your long voyage, crowning you with happiness and Comfort, when it has been completed.

You say one motive for directing your decision is the reflection of being so much nearer to your Father! - this tho' literally true, according to the Topography of the

Globe, it is virtually as far as London, where you may be now situated, for I have no more chance of ever setting Eyes on you again, than had you remained in England and to that prospect I must reconcile an eternal adieu, as you have done.

Amongst the many arguments which have impressed my Mind, on this important decision, is one in particular, - I feel no claim on Mr Campbell, to be burthened with my family, much less to interfere with him in any pecuniary way whatever, and I am not fully satisfied in my own mind that the warmth of your Aunt Eliza's affection may not have urged that in which I do not feel any encouragement to confide, by the conduct of Mr C. from whom I have never had a line these four years even to say his Wife had left him and if it should prove that he has been misguided by any prejudices adverse to my reputation or interest, I would have sooner suffered Martyrdom than believe my Daughters, placed as unexpected or unwelcome guests on him, or as intruders on his family while their own Father and Natural protector was alive! - I acknowledge however, that I reason thus from conjecture, chiefly, & I shall be glad to find myself mistaken as your fate has been resolved on.

Let me now suppose that you arrived in Calcutta and contrast the scene of perpetual Society by which you will be surrounded, with the course of life you have been accustomed to, - surrounded by the lightly, gay and tripping Lotharios of the place, some rational and worthy subjects, but the greater part unmatured by your experience and creatures made up of Vanity and self conceit, all flattering and talking a profusion of pretty things to please themselves, - and let me entreat you not to be hurried into any exchanges of confidence that may not be sanctioned by your Aunt's privity and concurrence. - I say so much because it is impossible for a person who has never been in India to form an opinion of the state of Society that exists in it, where the Circle is large - as well as expensive, and so much more free than in England on the part of the Men, that their assidualities generally turn the eager fancies of their young female associates in a few weeks, and I have frequently seen the most pleasant charming English Girls become completely Indian fine ladies within that time, or give their confidence where they may have had reason to repent it. In all these matters your Aunt will doubtless regulate the conduct of you both, if you will but attend to her, which I cannot too strongly enjoin.

The next subject for your attention is Expence. - The revolution of Parties, Balls etc etc and particularly in the Cold Season, is so rapid that any young woman living in a genteel family which forms a part of the first Circle, is hurried on by the intoxication of amusement and Varieties of Fancy in her dress, 'till forgetting she is not on equal terms with her protectress, in point of resource, the most extravagant and imprudent Bills have been run up at Europe Shops & with Milliners, - unable to satisfy these they must fall on the friend they live with, or attach disgracefully to them, when they marry, as a burthen on their husbands! who unsuspicious of the load, is naturally influenced by the most unfavorable impressions, which often lead to future want of confidence & breach of Conjugal affection. - but if it should so happen that the young woman does not Marry quickly, what are the consequences? - inward lamentation, self reproach and torment, - or - perhaps she is induced to rush into some imprudent connection that will disengage her from the horrors she endures.

I repeat , that you have no claims on Mr Campbell's purse - and you must know that the situation I am placed in is so circumscribed that it will not bear extravagance of any kind, your conduct must therefore be regulated by a due reflection on what I have pictured before, and that prudent consideration for my circumstances which I rest in confidence you will not fail to exert. When you arrive in India we shall endeavour to make some arrangements that may be permanent & decisive.

I have often wished you were to come in the China Ship by this route, where I should have the satisfaction of seeing you for a Month or six weeks while the Ship remained here, but as she could only take you as far as Poolo Penang, you would be obliged to find package from there to Bengal in another Ship, and that would be both troublesome and expensive; - besides, the visitation for so short a time would only open the Springs of remembrance and affection, to be repressed with a double sense of anguish and regret at separation, and as fate has determined that we cannot live together in the same Country, - it is better as it is.

I sincerely lament the melancholy situation in which your Aunt Fanny has pictured herself to be placed, to which every relief in my power shall be administered, and I hope she will yet find comfort - she sets her face against visiting me, and in as far as that objection rests on quitting friends she has been brought up with to associate with a Brother she has no recollection of, I can make great allowances, but if she should resolve on coming out, nothing would give either Mrs Perreau or myself more pleasure. - You are both most deeply bound in gratitude to her for her kind care and protection as well as education, and I rely on it, you have grateful hearts, to acknowledge it.

You will come out with advantages and an introduction to Society, as well as the manners of the world, which few young ladies who visit India can boast; and on the experience you will have derived from her tender and prudent introduction to these benefits, I place much dependence on your future happiness and welfare.

I was very ill when I received your Letter and so was your Mother-in-Law who has continued ill for some months, I bless God, she is now recovering daily, and that I am stouter and better than I have been for a very long while. We have another little Brother for you, Master Charley, and a sweet little infant he is; little Emma is a perfect beauty and as mild fancy can picture. - Marianne a stout pretty dimpled round faced arch but pretty girl with all, and Montague all life spirit & activity, - all are well however and what Robert may have written you all I cannot tell, but I never saw him better, nor has his finger ailed to my knowledge these five years! - he is nevertheless lazy beyond description, and his indolence has thrown him into Charles Salmon's way a situation he had at his command had he thought proper to deserve it. I mean the promise made me by Mr Parry, that he should recommend him to Mr Parker his Successor, to fill up the office of Resident at Croee, when Mr Browne leaves it, a few months hence, by which he may at least make £2000 pr ann: - this is the second pail of milk he has kicked down, and he sits grumbling at his Fortune, because he only gets about £225 a year, which he does not earn positively, and tho' he has my Table, he is always in difficulty. - I have got him a grant of Land however, in hopes of making a planter of him & interesting his mind by some object, - which I think has improved him a little. Still there is a precocity about his conduct, ill befitting his present age, which makes me very uneasy. Society seems almost his aversion, & when he is brought into it either sits mum - chance or duty the joke against him, in a manner that rather increases than diminishes the diffidence which so unfortunately influences his general Conduct. - He said he should write you but whether he has or not, I cannot tell.

I conclude this Epistle my dear Girls by wishing you a safe and speedy passage across the Seas, and uniting the unbounded affectionate regards of Mrs P with those of

Your ever affectionate Father
R S Perreau

Appendix B1

Accounts of 'Botany Bay' plantation sent with Letter 3, October 1823

A list of Slaves on Botany Bay Plantation with general monthly account of the expenditure of rice & wages -

No.	Names	Remarks etc.	bs. rice	Drs.	S.
1	Scrub	Head man	6	1	"
"	Greta dos. wife	Takes care of Spices	6	1	"
"	Benantallam child to Do.	Nut gatherer	3	"	2
"	Baga Baja	Too infirm for work	6	1	"
5	Mandan Dos. son	Works at the hoe	6	1	2
"	Dupal Dos. mother	Nut gatherer, infirm	6	"	2
"	Leusie leusie	Works at the hoe	6	1	"
"	Oubie oubie	Too infirm for work	6	"	3
"	Doodoo	Nut gatherer	3	"	1
10	Iiah Debtor	Works at the hoe	7	1	"
"	Trim	do.	7	1	"
"	Omer	Nut gatherer	6	1	"
"	Mpoumin	do.	3	"	2
14	Gamboe	do.	3	"	1
		Total	72	11	1
		My own Servants			
"	Harry	Horse boy	6	1	"
16	Gylar	Wating boy	3	"	2

Iiah's debt will be liquidated at the end of the year, when it will be necessary to get another hand as three hands at the hoe are not sufficient to keep the plantation in a good state of cultivation, two of the above list are too infirm for work, 4 of the nut gatherers are children and the other 2 are getting old but still capable of doing work; and I think it would be advisable to emancipate both Baja baja & Oubie oubie.

Wm. G. Day.

Appendix B2

Mr. William Grant Day in Account

Dr.

Assumed charge of Botany Bay Plantation on the 1st. Dec. 1823 with Spices, Slaves etc

To Cash

Jan 21	Received from Mr.P. Neish the amount sale of Spices on assuming charge vitz.		
"			
	To 53 lbs. of mace at 3 succoos per lb.	P. 39. 3. "	
	" 106 lbs. No.1 Nutmegs at ditto	79. 2. "	
	To 74 lbs. No.2 ditto at 2 succoos per lb.	37. " "	156. 1.

Amount carried forward P.156. 1. "

Current with Charles Day, Esquire, 1823

Cr.

By Cash paid for the following articles on assuming charge of the Plantation vitz			
		Drs. s. p.	Drs. s. p.
Dec. 1822	By 21 nutmeg plants large and small	4. 2 "	
	" Carting ditto	" 2 "	
	" 50 small nutmeg plants	6 2 "	
	" Carting ditto	" 2 "	
	" Manure 15 cart loads at 10 lds. per P	1 2 "	
	" 5 new spice basketts	1 " "	14. 2. "
Disbursements in January 1823			
Jan. 5	By 3 bags of Rice for Plantation at P.3.1 per bag	9. 3. "	
	" 1 spade for ditto	1. 2. "	
31	" Carting manure 3 loads for ditto	1. " "	1. " "
Disbursements in February 1823			
Feb. 6	By 3 bags of rice for Plantation P3.1 per bag	9. 3. "	
	" Carting ditto	" 2. "	
8	" 8 loads of manure	2. " "	
	" A grass knife	" 1. "	
10	" Carting manure 16 loads at 10 lds.pr.P.	1. 2 "	
	" ditto 4 ditto 3 ditto	1. 1. "	
15	" Wages to people	7. 1. "	
17	" 7 loads of manure	2. " "	
	" A buffaloe & Cart	50. " "	
26	" 1 bundle of rattans	" 1 "	74. 3 "
Amount brought forward			P 101. 2. "
Balance carried over			54. 3."
	Current Dollars		156. 1."

Appendix B3

Mr. William Grant Day in A

Dr.

		P. s. p.	P. s. p.
To Cash			
To balance brought forward			54. 3. "
May 12	Received from Mr. W.T.Lewis the amount Sale of Spices		60. 2. "
	Carried forward	P.	115. 1. "

with Charles Day, Esquire, 1823

Cr.

			P. s. p.	P. s. p.
	Disbursements in March 1823			
March 1	By 6 bags of rice for two months use at 2p.3s. per bag.	P.	16. 2. "	
	" Wages to people		7. 1. "	
	Hire of manure per month		2. " "	
5	" repairing wheels of buffaloe cart		" 2 "	
30	" property tax on the plantation quarter from the 1 October. 1822 to 31 Jany. /23		2. 1 "	28. 1. "
	Disbursements in April 1823			
April 1	By wages to people	P.	7. 1. "	
15	" buffaloe rope		" 1 "	
19	" hire of manure pr. month		" " "	9. 2. "
	Disbursements in May 1823			
May 1	By 3 bags of rice for people at P3.1 per bag	P.	9. 3. "	
	" Wages to people		7. 1. "	
5	" hire for manure per month		2. " "	
	" 1 spade		2. " "	
12	" 250 bamboes at P2.1 per 100 bs.		6. 1. "	27. 1. "
	Disbursements in June 1823			
June 1	By 3 bags of rice at 3.2 per bag		10. 2. "	
4	" Wages to people		7. 1 "	
8	" Repairing buffaloe cart		4. " "	
	" cart hire for rice, the buffaloe being stolen		" 2 "	
16	" hire of manure per month		2 " "	24. 1. "
	Disbursements for July 1823			
July 4	By 3 bags of rice at P3.2 per bag	P.	10. 2. "	
	" Wages to people		7. 1. "	
	" Cart hire for rice		" 2 "	
7	" hire of manure per month		2. " "	20. 1. "
	Amount brought forward		P.	109. 3. "

Appendix B4

Mr. William Grant Day in Account

Dr.

	P.s.p.	P.s.p.
Balance brought forward		5. 2. "
To Cash		
Received from Cursedjie, Munsedjie the amt. Sale of Spices vitz.		
2 Peculs & 4 Catties of nutmegs at 80 P. per pecul	163. " "	
87 lbs. of mace at 80 P. per pecul	52. " "	215. " "
Total Amount	P.	220. 2. "
Balance brought forward	P.	15. " "
To Cash		
Received from Messrs Pat Neish & Co. Ltd., amount sale of spices vitz.		
214 lbs. of nutmegs at 100P per pecul	153. 2. "	
35 " mace ditto	41. 2. "	195. " "
Total	P	210. " "
Balance	P.	181. 1. "
	Errors	Excepted

Fort Marlbro
31 Decr. 1823

Current with Charles Day, Esquire, 1823

Cr.

		P.s. p.		P. s. p.
	Disbursements in August 1823			
Aug. 4.	By 3 Bags of rice at P.4 per bag	12. " "		
	" Wages to people	9. " "		
6	" Hire of manure per mensem	2. " "		
	" A Debtor See Iiah for the plantation	20. " "		43. " "
	Disbursements in September 1823			
Sept. 1	By 4 bags of rice at 4p. per bag	16 " "		
	" Wages to people 9. " "			
5	" Hire for manure per month	2. " "		27. 2. "
	Disbursements in October 1823			
Oct. 1	By 4 bags of rice at P4. per bag	16. " "		
	" Wages to people	9. " "		
20 "	" 3,000 attops for house on plantation at P.14 per thousand	42. " "		
	" 2 bundles of rattans	1. " "		
22	" Hire of manure per month	2. " "	70. 2. "	
	Disbursements in November 1823			
Nov. 6	By 4 bags of rice ar 4P. per bag	16. " "		
	" Wages to people	9. " "		
9	" hire for manure per month	2. " "		
	" 6 cart loads of manure at 3 lds. per Dr.	2. " "		
15	" 50 planks for Stables at 25 Drs. per 100	12. 2. "		
	" 3 timbers for ditto at P1. per timber	3. 3. "		
18	" posts for ditto at 1 R's per post	1. 2. "		
	" rattans 4 bundles for ditto	1. "	"	
	" 35 bamboos for ditto	2. "	"	
21	" contract for building ditto	12. " "		64. " "
	Total Amount		P.	205. 2. "
	Disbursements in the month Decr. 1823			
Dec. 1	By 4 bags of rice at 4 ½ per bag P.	18. " "		
	" wages to people	11. 1. "		
6	" monthly hire for manure	2. " "		31. 1.
	Total P.			31. 1.

Appendix C1

and Rice Abstract of Combong Plantation
:losed in letter dated 10th November 1825)

Names	Rice	Pay		Remarks
Men	Bs.	Drs.	s.	
Nela	6		2	There is a coffree/named
Kabalu	6		2	Ioogie/ not included in this
See Alu	6		2	list, as he has inter married
Kavaw	6		2	with a woman of Bogles
Dapet	6		2	at his Cobone barree, he is
Gido	6		2	to give a substitute which
Brush	6		2	makes our number 20.
Lambiguy	6		2	
Goya	6		2	
Bangia	6		2	
Women				
Rende	6		2	
Govi	6		2	
Capasi	6		2	
Combong	6		2	
Bungo	6		2	
Children				
Gylar	6		2	
Rumah	4		1	
See Tom	4		1	
See Oocho	4		1	
	Bs. 108	15	3	

e has 17 of his own / extra to our own twenty / people at present upon the plantation / so he says / however I doubt it. twenty hands belonging to the concern are quite sufficient for Combong. The extra hands increase the expences e plantation to 192 Bs of Rice and 32 Drs.

rage produce from 1822/ to 24.

s	Nuts	Remarks
	262590)	
	)	
	333938)	Which average 896 nuts daily
	)	
	385565)	
	Cloves	
	Bamboes	
	- -	Mr. Bogle has not for this yr given any acct of Cloves.
	1049 ¾	
	916	

e has got this year 1825 upwards of 2,000 Bs. of Cloves, in / 22 he must have had a similar crop, as we have every third a superior crop to the two last for which reason he did not put the quantity of Cloves / at least I conclude so / verage from 30 to 40 bamboes of wet cloves when cured to be equal to a pecul.

Appendix C2

Enclosed in letter dated 10th November 1825. Endorsed - Estimate of Botany Bay Plantation.

Statement of property belongin

ESTATE	Number of Trees	Amt. produce of nutmegs	Ditto of Mace	Value per Annum	Annual Expence
BOTANY BAY					
	Trees	Pls.	Pls.	Drs.	Drs
	600	12	3	1,500	180

I WILLIAM GRANT DAY
income and expence of the plantation herein enumerated
is to the best of my knowledge and belief just and fair

Fort Marlbro
8th August, 1825

to William Grant Day

'et Income r annum	Value of Cattle	Value of house and out offices	Value of the plantn. at 6 yrs. purchase	Remarks
'rs.	Drs.	Drs.	Drs.	
320	200	1,500	7,920	

do solemnly swear before God and the Holy Evangelist that the above Statement of produce, is a true and fair account, that the value affixed to the house and cattle

Signed / Wm. G. Day

Sworn to before me this 8 day of August, in the Year of Our Lord
One thousand eight hundred and twenty five

Sd. John Prince
Late Ag. Test

/ A true copy /

Appendix C3

List of Slaves belonging to Combong Plantation the joint property of Chas. Day & Robt. Bogle transferred by John Prince Esqre. 1st Jany, 1814.

Names	County.	Employt.	Wages	Rice	Remarks
Males			Drs. s.c.		
Pompey	Neas	Gourdan	1 2 "	8 Bs.	This man married to Nan a Batta woman has 2 children a boy Pa girl named Sack and Romana all had the small pox 1816 1 child more / a girl / dead, 1820 1 Boy dead /
Bugulo	do.	Cartman	1 2 "	8 "	This man married to Cumbang a Batta woman has one boy named Gaila, this man died of the s.pox 1816
Sabu	do.	Cattle kr.	1 2 "	8 "	This man married to Embas a Batta no children had the s.pox 1815. Both murdered by Se Dapet Gido & harry, the last of whom was hanged for it on March 1816.
Nela	do.	Labourer	" 2 "	8 "	This man married to See Bungo a Batta has a son named Tom had the s.pox 1816.
Cafetu	do.	do.	1 " "	8 "	This man married to Capad a neas woman no children had the s.pox. This man died in hospital of wounds received in defending himself from some Moosie men who carried off Untong.
Careti	do.	do.	" 2 "	8 "	This man married to Rindo a Batta has a daughter named Govi Govi had the S.pox. This man came under the lash of the law by attempting to murder Kate banished to Nattal 1821.
Kabulos	do.	A.Ce.Keepr.	1 " "	6 "	Had the small pox 1816
See Alu Labu	do.	Labourr.	" 2 "	6 "	Ditto do.
Kavau	do.	do.	" 2 "	6 "	Ditto when young
Dupi	do.	do.	" 2 "	6 "	Ditto 1816 To be worked on the roads for 2 years in Irons for the murder of Sabu 1818 released and is married to a slave woman of Mr. Bogles named See Tvia.
Cido	do.	do.	" 2 "	6 "	Had the smallpox to be worked on the roads in irons for the murder of Sabu released 1818 married to Govi Govi.

rush	Neas	Labourr.	" 2 "	6 "	Had the small pox
ntong	do.	do.	" 2 "	6 "	Ditto. This man carried off by Musi people & sold beyond the hills 1817.
eter	Batta	do.	" 2 "	6 "	Marked with the small pox but took the desease a 2nd time and died Feby.1816
abbiguy	do.		1 " "	6 "	Had the small pox 1816
abu	Neas	Cartman	1 " "	6 "	Married to Cumbong on the death of Bagalu had the s.pox 1816.
oya	do.	Labourer	" 2 "	6 "	This man was a slave of Jas. Bogles Estate mortgaged to C. Day now transferred to Combong. C.D. & R.B. paid P.65 for him bide A/C CD & RB.
aruka	do.	do.	" 2 "	6 "	Ditto ditto ditto Married a slave woman of Mr. Bogles / a Ryang / named Ramat
angai	Bali	do.	" 2 "	6 "	Ditto ditto ditto
uja	Nes	do.	" 2 "	6 "	Ditto ditto ditto Run to Musi 1818

umber of trees	Nutmegs	1,100 full bearing
	Cloves	500 do.
	Nutmegs	200 just planted
	Cloves	300 do.
do. Cattle		10 all old

o carts or implements of husbandry.

ist of Slaves continued

emales			Drs.	s. c.	
an	Batta	Labourr.	" 2 "	6 "	Married to Pompey / had the s.pox / children 3, 2 boys and a girl.
umbang	do.	do.	" 2 "	6 "	Married to Sabu on the death of Bagalu / 1 boy Gaila
mbas	do.	do.	" 2 "	6 "	Married to Sabu / had the s.pox 1816 / this woman murdered with her husband by Dape Gido & Harry a slave of Mr. Bogles who was hung 1816
unga	do.	do.	" 2 "	6 "	Married to Nela / had the S.pox/ this woman a lunatic
a Parti	do.	do.	" 2 "	6 "	Married to a slave of Mr. Bogles named See Braka on the death of Ca Fieto.
indi	do.	do.	" 2 "	6 "	Married to Carati had the S.pox.

Appendix D1

Abstract State of Monthly Expenditure of Rice and Belangio at Combong Plantation

No.	Names	Occupation	Rice		B	
			Bs.	Co.	Rs.	Aa
1	See Bracas	Toukan	6	"	1	8
"	Brush	At the hoe	6	"	1	"
"	Jala	do.	6	"	1	"
"	Gaigie	do.	6	"	1	"
"	Dapet	do.	6	"	1	"
"	Kavowlee	do.	6	"	1	"
"	Narram	do.	6	"	2	"
"	Gylah	Ploughman	6	"	2	"
"	Kalure	do.	6	"	2	"
"	Gidoh	Cartman	6	"	1	8
"	Jalu	Tree Pruner	6	"	1	"
"	Daugie	At the hoe	6	"	1	"
"	Gaga	Invalid	6	"	1	"
"	Navow	Cattle Keeper	6	"	2	"
"	Imee	In charge of the house	6	"	2	"
"	Buyong Katek	Nut gatherer	6	"		8
17 "	Gunuyon	do.	6	"		8
		WOMEN				
1 "	Teera	Nut gatherer	6	"	1	"
"	Panorattee	do.	6	"	1	"
"	Rendet	do.	6	"	1	"
"	Bunghe	do.	6	"	1	"
"	Gove	do.	6	"	1	"
"	Rama	do.	6	"	1	"
"	Combong	do.	6	"	1	"
"	Judi	do.	6	"	1	"
"	Cappassee	do.	6	"	1	"
"	Inian	do.	6	"	1	"
"	Nelly	do.	6	"	1	"
"	Selama Moadok	do.	6	"	1	"
"	Sally	do.	6	"	1	"
	Gungeram (Burgalee)	Cattle Keeper	8	"	8	"
"	Samet	Gourdan	6	"	4	"
"	Sait	Jantoolis			10	
	Two extra hands for cleaning and taking care of Sice on Combong at R's 2 ea.				4	
	To 10 bags of Margey Rice averaging two pr. bag at R's 10 pr bag				100	
		Total	194	"	162	

Bencoolen
1st April 1827

A true Abstract

Wm. G. Day

Appendix D2

Endorsed: Ac/Ct. Chas. Day. Esq., Bencoolen, 3rd Aug. 1827

CHARLES DAY ESQR. in ACCOUNT CURRENT with WM. GRANT DAY

1826	To the wages of a Jantoolis from Nov. 1825 to Nov. 1826 at 10 rupees pr month	120. 0. 0	
	To ditto 2 Extra hands for taking care of spice form Nov. 1825 to Nov. /26 at 2 rupees per mo	48. “ “	
	To basketts for drying spice	5 “ “	
	To half share of a smoking house	159 “ “	
Nov. 1	To 10 Bags of Bengal Rice at 10 Rs pr bag 1 qr.	100. 0. 0	
15	To peoples wages on plantation 1 qr	48. “ “	
	Jantoolis ditto	10. “ “	
	To 2 Extra hands for taking care of Spice 1 qr.	4. “ “	162 “ “
Dec. 28	To burying See Goya a slave		6 “ “
	“ Jantoolis wages	10 “ “	
	“ 2 Extra hands for taking care of spice	4 “ “	
			14 “ “
1827			
Jan. 5	“ Expences of plantation as on November		162 “ “
	“ Attops for patching dwelling house		4 “ “
Feby. 1	“ Jantoolis wages	10 “ “	
Mar 11	“ 10 bags of Bengal rice at 10 Rs per bag	100 “ “	
	“ 2 Extra hands for taking care of spice	4 “ “	114 “ “
	“ People's wages on plantation	48 “ “	
	“ Jantoolis wages	10 “ “	
	“ 2 Extra hands for taking care of spice	4 “ “	62

1825		
Nov.16	By Spices delivered to Mr. Baskett viz.	
	Nutmegs good weighing lbs 374	
	ditto inferior “ “ 105	
	Mace good “ 99	
1826 Sepr. 6	By Spices delivered to Mr. Baskett viz	
	Nutmegs good weighing lbs 237	
	ditto inferior “ lbs 93	
	Mace good “ 107	
Dec. 8	“ Sale of one pecul of Nutmegs at ps 60 pr pecul	120.
1827		
Jany 15	“ Sale of 48 cloves to Baba Mingo at Rs 180 per pecul	64 “
Mar. 29	“ Spices delivered to Mr. Baskett viz	
	Nutmegs wg. lbs. 273 good	
	Mace “ “ 103 do.	
	Nutmegs “ 95 infr.	
June 8	“ Amount sales of five peculs of cloves at ps 5 per pecul	650
Aug. 1	“ 20 peculs of Cloves on hand not yet delivered to Mr. Baskett	
	“ 3 Peculs of Nutmegs ditto ditto	
	“ 1 ditto of Mace	
Aug. 3	By balance at this date carr. fwd.	834.
		964.
		1799

/Contd.

	Bt. fwd.		856 " "		
Mar 11	To Clothing for ½ of the plantation at Rs 8 per man /on all 34 men/ ½ share 17 men		136 " "		
	To ditto your ½ share of 2000 attops for dwelling house at 24 rupees per 1000		24 " "		
April 1	To Jantoolis wages	10. " "			
	" 2 Extra hands for taking care of spice	4 " "	14 " "		
May 7	" expences of plantation for the present month		162 " "		
	" drying matts and baskets for cloves		8 " "		
	" paid Coolies for picking 560 bamboos of Cloves at six bamboos per rupee		93 8 "		
June 11	" paid Jantoolis wages	10 " "			
	" 2 Extra hands for taking care of spice	4 " "	14 " "		
	" ditto Coolies for packing 873 bamboos of Cloves at six bamboos per rupee		145 8 "		
July 8	" 10 bags Bengal rice and other expences for the month including wages etc.		162 " "		
Aug 3	" paid Jantoolis wages	10 " "			
	" 2 Extra hands for taking care of spice	4 " "	14 " "		
	" 20 Pecul Boxes for Cloves at 7 rs pr box		140 " "		
	" Clamping marking etc ditto at 7 ru. per do.		20 " "		
	Rupees		1799 " "	Rupees	1799 " "

Bencoolen 3rd August 1827 Per Borneo Wm. G. Day.

Appendix D3

List of Slaves belonging to Combong given by Mr. B.

1 See Dangin
" Aclah
" Dapet
" Manttek
" Sabu
" Kavow
" Geedoh
" Tom bayam (with Mr. B.)
" Brush
10 " Buyong Katek
" Ucho-ocho
" Gylah
" Goyah) Dead of the
" Krutah) cholerah
15 Injai pemjang with Mr. B.

Men
Mr .Bogle's people at work at Combong Names

Samet)
Kaluang) Males
Kahjie)

See Atoe)
" Ramat) Females
3 Coffrees)

Women

See Capassi
" Rendot
" Combong
" Bungak
" Govi-govi
20 " Rhumah (with Mr. B.)

(A true memo)

Wm. G. Day.

Appendix E1

Charles Day Esqre. in Accot.

Dr.

–

			Rs.	As/s	1
1827					
Aug. 3rd	To balance to date		964	5	3
Sept. 8th	To paid peoples wages including the wages of a Jantooliss & two extra hands for taking care of spice at Combong, for two months	48. 8			
	9 bags of Bengal rice @ Ts 10 pr bag	90 "	138	8	"
Octbr. 10	Paid duties on 20 peculs of Cloves shipped pr. Schooner Helen	190	"		
	Mace shipped per ditto	38 11	288	11	"
	Ditto for boat hire wharfage on ditto		16	"	"
Nov. 15	To paid peoples wages for October as pr. Abstract		138	8	"
19	To do. freight on 22 cases shipped per Helen for Singapore @ Ts. 30 pr. ton at 4 cases to the ton equal to 5 ½ tons Sa. Rs. 165 equal to guilders at an exchange of 19 pr. cent.		198	7	"
Dec. 31	To charge for Smoaking produce from Nov. / 25 to the month of Octbr./28 (both inclusive) being 2 yrs. & 11 mths at Ts 4 pr month. account This charge omitted in former account		140	"	"
1828					
Jan. 5	To paid ½ share of peoples clothing for the present year @ TS 6 per man (vide abstract, 24 hands)		96	"	"
15	Pd people's wages for Decr. as pr Abstract		138	8	"
March 18	To Pd. people's wages for Febyas pr Abstract		138	8	"
April 15	To paid for a cart and buffaloe on joint Acct @ Ts 80 ½ share		40	"	"
May 10	To paid peoples wages for April as pr Abstract		138	"	"
do. 31	To charge for smoaking produce for March & April & May @ Ts 4 pr month		12	"	"
	Guilders		2385	15	4

Errors Excepted

Wm. G. Day.

1827

Novr.20th By produce placed in the hands of Messrs Gutherie & Clark, Singapore to be transmited to Europe to the care of Messrs Morris & Rennie, London viz.

20 pecul cases of Cloves marked C.D.
1 case of Nutmegs ditto wg lbs 370

1 ditto Mace " " 157

Decr. 31st By memo. Gave over charge of produce to Mr. Baskett from 1st Novr. 27 to 29th Feby. 28 during the time of my absence at Singapore.

May 31st By balance to date 2805. 15 4
Guilders 2385. 15. 4

Bencoolen pr Helen 31st May 1828

Appendix E2

Abstract of Pay & Rice issued monthly to the labourers on Combong for 1827/28

	Bs.	Rs.	As.
MALES			
See Brush	6	1	"
Lala	6	1	"
Gaigie	6	1	"
Dapet	6	1	"
Kavowlu	6	1	"
Gylah	6	1	"
Kaluang	6	2	"
Gidoh	6	2	"
Galu	6	1	8
Dangin	6	1	"
Kasettel	6	1	"
Travow	6	2	"
Buyong Katet	3	"	8
Ochi ochi	4	"	8
FEMALES			
See Beaumiattu	6	1	"
Rendet	6	1	"
Govi	6	1	"
Rumah	6	1	"
Combong	6	1	"
Papassee	6	1	"
Lanret Madoh	6	1	"
Sally	6	1	"
Lamet (overseer)	6	4	"
Sait (Jantoolis)	"	6	"
Cattle Keeper	8	8	"
See Iiah & wife taking care of spice A.B. for 2 mths.	24	4	"
Total Bms.	177	48	8

(True Abstracts)
Wm. G. Day.

Abstract of monthly produce at Combong the month of May 1826 to 31st April 1828

Nuts gathered in	May 1826	7034
do do	June "	8120
do do	July "	9330
do do	Augt. "	7624
do do	Septr. "	8950
do do	Octr. "	8520
do do	Novr. "	8590
do do	Decr. "	6490
do do	Jany. 1827	6744
do do	Feby. "	7780
do do	March "	8040
do do	April "	9590
do do	May "	8310
do do	June "	15100
do do	July "	9520
do do	Aug. "	5060
do do	Septr. "	6635
do do	Octr. "	14714
Recd by Mr. Baskett	Novr. "	"
do do	Decr.	"
do do	Jany. 1828	"
do do	Feby. "	"
Nuts gathered by me	March "	5160
do do	April "	2860

Bibliography

Bakewell, S. *The Smart,* Chatto & Windus 2001

Bastin, J.S. *The British in West Sumatra 1685-1825*, University of Malaya, Kuala Lumpur 1965

Bence-Jones, M. *Clive Of India*, 1974

Cambridge University, Alumni

Collis, M . *Raffles*, Faber and Faber 1966

Day Family Papers, in possession of Mrs P N Barker

Day, J.T. *The Origins of Francis Day, Founder of Fort St George (Madras)*, Genealogists' Magazine, Vol 28, No. 7, 2005

Day, J.Wentworth, *Harvest Adventure*, Harrap & Co 1946

Dictionary of National Biography, Oxford University Press

East India Company, *The English Factories In India, 1618-1669*, ed W. Foster, 13 vols, 1906-27

East India Company, *The English Factories in India 1670-1677*, ed. C. Fawcett, 2vols, 1936

East India Company, *Court Minutes Books, 1618-1679*, ed. N. Sainsbury 1862-1892

Eton College, Alumni

Furber, H. John *Company at Work*, 1970

Gardner, B. *The East India Company*, Rupert Hart-Davis 1971

Gentleman's Magazine 1746

Grey, C. *Merchant Venturers of London* 1923

Griffith, G. *Men Who Have Made Empire*, C Arthur Pearson 1899

Harleian Society, *Visitation of Bershire* 1623

Hickey, W. *Memoirs of William Hickey*, ed. A. Spencer, 1913-1925, vol. 4, pp.324, 449

Howard, D.S. *Chinese Armorial Porcelain*, Faber and Faber 1974

Howard, D. S. *Chinese Armorial Porcelain*, Vol II, Heirloom & Howard 2003

Keay, J. *The Honourable Company*, Harper Collins 1991

Lyall, A. *The Rise and Expansion of British Dominion in India*, John Murray 1894

Merchant Taylors School, Alumni

Spear, P. *History of India*, 1965

Spear, P. *The Nabobs*, Oxford University Press 1963

Sutton, J. *Lords of the East, The East India Company and its Ships*, Conway Maritime Press 1981

Vicar General, Marriage Licences

Wagner, Sir A. *English Genealogy*, Clarendon Press 1960

Wild, A. *The East India Company*, Harper Collins, 1999

Woodruff, P. *Men Who Ruled India*, Vol I The Founders, Jonathan Cape 1953

Wurtzberg, C. E. *Raffles of the Eastern Isles*, 1954

Index

A

Achin xli
Allas xxviii
Amherst 62, 115
Anderson 10, 33
Armagon xvii

B

Bantam xvii, xxviii
Baskett , William , 22, 29, 30, 35, 44-46, 51, 52, 54, 59, 60, 62, 64, 67, 68, 71-73, 79, 89, 90, 97, 98, 101, 104, 109, 110, 113, 143
Batavia xxxvi, 17, 27, 28, 35, 50, 66, 68, 70, 82, 91, 94, 103
Batavian Society of Arts xl
Bell 32, 46, 114
Bencoolen i-iii, vii, viii, xi, xv, xxvii, xxxi-xxxvi, xxxix, xl, xlii-xliv, 3, 7, 9, 12, 17, 18, 21, 27-31, 33-35, 37, 38, 40, 42, 44, 46, 49, 50, 51, 53, 54, 56, 57, 59, 62-66, 68-72, 74, 75, 77, 78, 80, 82, 84, 85, 87-89, 94, 97, 99, 103-105, 107, 108, 110, 111, 113-115, 117, 118, 136, 138, 139, 143
Bengal xxv, xxxii, 3, 15, 17, 20, 31, 34, 35, 50, 60, 78, 85, 94, 114, 117, 121, 138, 139, 143
Benturin(g) 4,18, 25, 26, 29, 31'
Bevis Hill xxxii, xliii, 11, 38, 39, 47, 55, 64, 74, 76, 81, 83, 88, 98, 105, 112
Black Book xix, xxiv
Bogle 4-6, 13-16, 18, 20-22, 26, 29-31, 44, 45, 47, 50-52, 59, 60, 63, 64, 67, 70, 72-75, 78, 79, 87, 89, 90, 92, 94-96, 113, 131, 134, 140
Bombay xix, xxiii, xxv, xxvii, xxviii, xliv
Boone xxiii, xxiv
Boone, Charles xxiii, xxiv
Boone, Thomas xxiii
Botany Bay ix, x, xliv, 5, 9, 13, 18, 28, 43, 44, 45, 49, 51, 53, 57, 59, 61, 64-67, 70, 73, 95, 96, 123, 125, 132
Botany House 5
Botolph Wharf xxiii, xxiv
Braham 115, 117

C

Calcutta xxxiii, xxxvi, 3, 29, 32, 38, 49, 54, 56, 59, 71, 74, 79, 94, 98, 110, 114, 117, 119
Calicut xxvi
Canning 115
Canton xxv

China xi, xxv, xxvi, xxix, xxxvi, xli, 113, 114, 121
Claridge 85, 88, 100
Clive xx, 146
Clive, Robert xx
cloth worker xvii
cloves xxviii, 14, 61, 78, 94, 115, 131, 138, 139
Combong ix, x, xliv, 13, 15, 20, 21, 29, 37, 44, 45, 49, 52, 53, 59-61, 64, 66, 67, 70, 72, 73, 78, 87, 89-94, 96, 100, 104, 107, 109, 131, 134-136, 140, 143-145
Cooper xxxii, 114
Cornwallis xxvi

D

Davy, Sir Humphrey xlii
Day iii-xi, xv-xx, xxiv, xxvi, xxviii, xxix, xxxii, xxxiv, xxxvii, xlii-xlv, 3, 8, 9, 12, 13, 15-18, 22-27, 35, 37, 39, 46, 47, 49, 55-59, 61, 63, 65, 66, 68-70, 75-77, 81-84, 86-88, 101, 102-108, 112-114, 117, 123, 125, 127, 129, 132, 134-136, 138-140, 143, 144, 146
Day, Charles vi, vii, xvi, xxvi, xxxii, xxxiv, xliii, xliv, xlv, 3, 13, 57, 77, 102, 103, 106-108, 112-114, 117, 125, 127, 129, 143
Day, Francis xv-xix, xlv, 146
Day, Robert xix, xx, xxiii, xxiv, xxvi
Day, Thomas (son of Robert) xvi, xxv, xxvi
Day, Thomas Skottowe ix, xvi, xxvii, xxxii, xlii, xliii, 9-12, 22, 24, 25, 31, 32, 35, 40, 43, 54, 55, 63, 64, 73
Day, William Grant ix, xv, xvi, xxvii, xxxii, xliii, xliv'
Dutch ix, x, xv, xxv, xxviii, xxxvi, xxxix, xli, xlii, xliii, xlv, 27, 28, 37-39, 42-44, 51, 53, 56, 62, 63, 66, 68, 78, 79, 83, 88, 111-113, 115

E

East India Company (EICo) xv-xvii, xix, xx, xxiii, xxiv, xxv, xxxii, 115, 146, 147
East India House xi, xxi, xxiii
Eton xvi, xvii, , 146

F

First General Voyage xviii
Fort Marlborough xv, xxvii, xxviii, xxxi-xxxiii, 13, 113-115, 117, 118
Fort St George xi, xviii, xxiv, xlv, 146

G

Gentleman's Magazine xxiv, , 146
Glifford, Elizabeth xxiv
Gordon 115
Grant, James 8, 42, 69, 72, 74, 79, 91, 98, 100, 110, 114

H

Halhead 25
Hastings, Lord Moira xli, 62, 115
Hastings, Warren xl
Hickey, William xxxiii, xlv, 146'
Huguenot xxxii

J

Janin, Incie xvi, 57'
Java xvii, xxviii, xxxvi, xxxix, xl, xlii, 79
Prince, John 78, 103, 113, 132, 134

L

Lamb, Charles xxiii
Lancaster 8

leeches 11
Lewis 10, 30, 35, 61, 68, 69, 72, 91, 97-99, 107, 108, 112, 114, 127

M

mace xxviii, 14, 31, 95, 125, 129
Mackenzie 48, 115'
Madras xi, xvi-xviii, xxii, xxxi, xxxii, xlv, 30, 117, 146
Malacca xxxvi, xlii, 28, 82, 85, 105, 108, 115

Malaya 146
Mark Lane xxv, xxvi
Matson xvii
Matson, Elizabeth xvii
Matson, Robert xvii
Merchant Taylors School xxvi, 147
Minto xxxvi

N

Napoleon xxxv, xxxvi, xl
Netherlands 72, 82
Nicholson 32, 33
nutmegs xxviii, 31, 61, 129, 132

O

opium ix, xv, xxxii, 7, 22, 29, 30, 38, 45, 52, 54, 56, 62, 79, 80, 113

P

Padang 28, 37, 44, 47, 49, 51, 74, 94, 105
Parry 118, 122
Penang xxxv, xxxvi, 64, 82, 85, 88, 105, 108, 114, 121
pepper xxviii, xxxi
Perreau x, xxxii, xxxiii, xlv, 8, 16, 22, 38, 45, 46, 54, 64, 68, 75, 81, 87, 100, 112-115, 117, 121, 122
Perreau, Daniel xxxiii
Perreau, Frances Mary 114
Perreau, Robert Samuel x, xxxii, xxxiii, 113-115, 117
Prince, John 78, 103, 113, 132, 134
Pulau Nias(s) xl, 114

R

Raffles, Stamford xi, xv, xxx, xxxiv-xxxvi, xxxix, xl, xli, xlii, 4, 10, 15, 18-20, 24, 32, 78, 113-115, 146, 147
Raja of Chandragiri xviii
Rudd xxxiii, xlv

S

Salmon 115, 117, 122
Salmond xlii, 9
San Thome xviii
Siddens 14
Siddons 114
Singapore x, xv, xli-xliii, 42, 49, 50, 64, 68, 69, 72, 75, 76, 81, 82, 85, 88, 95, 97, 103, 106, 108, 109, 112, 113, 143
Singapore Institute xlii, xliii

slaves xv, xxxix, xli, 5-7, 13-15, 54, 57, 59, 96, 113-115, 123, 124, 134, 135, 140
Southampton viii, xi, xxxii, xxxvii, xliv, xlv, 7, 46, 47
Spear Hall xxxii
spices x, 14, 31, 61, 72, 78, 79, 95, 97, 104, 106, 113, 129
spice plantation xv, 113
St Helena xl, xxxv
Suez xli
Sugar Concern 4, 29
Surat xvi, xviii, xix, xxvi, xxvii

T

Table Bay xxv
Trinity College, Cambridge xxvii

W

Wallingford xi, xix, 2
Wellesley xxxv, xxxvi
Wentworth, Helen xvi
Wentworth, Paul xvi
Westminster School xxxiii
Wilberforce, William xl
Williams 51, 57, 67, 71, 90
Winter 4, 18, 19, 25, 26, 41, 79, 100, 103, 104
Wren xxvii, xxviii

writers xx, 37, 43, 50, 52

Z

Zoological Society xlii

Lightning Source UK Ltd.
Milton Keynes UK
26 August 2009

143040UK00001B/1/P

9 781843 822028